W. GIFFORD-JONES, MD

What I Learned as a Medical Journalist

a collection of columns

ActNatural Corporation
5948 3rd Line RR#1
Hillsburgh, ON
N0B 1Z0

ISBN: 978-0-9867247-4-9

Copy Writing: W. Gifford-Jones, MD
Copy Editing: Susan F. Watts, RN, BScN
Cover Photo: Sam Truax
Book and Cover Design: Jasper van Meurs

Printed in Canada by Friesens Corp.

*Satisfaction of one's curiosity
is one of the greatest sources
of happiness in life.*

- Dr. Linus Pauling

Contents

Foreword

What did I learn as a medical journalist for the last 37 years? In one word – "plenty"! It's been a fascinating ride which I wouldn't have missed. My life since I first lifted a pen has been a life of deadlines, demands and pressures, somewhat like being married to a demanding nymphomaniac. Some weeks I would have preferred the nymphomaniac! But weekly deadlines help to focus the mind, and force one to see the forest as well as the trees.

It's been said that even stray dogs have their lucky days. I've been lucky throughout my life, but being admitted to The Harvard Medical School was prime and Lady Luck helped me to graduate. But what I say in this book has little to do with what I was taught at HMS. Ninety-nine percent has to do with what I learned from being a medical journalist. It provided the experience of interviewing outstanding medical authorities for many years and becoming involved in many medical issues, some exceedingly controversial.

But how did this second career, aside from my medical practice, begin? In 1956 I was surprised to find that many of my female patients knew practically nothing about gynecology and their own anatomy. So I penned my first book for their enlightenment. But my editor kept urging me to write a newspaper column. As a busy surgeon I kept resisting deadlines. I succumbed in 1975. I started writing a column as a hobby for the Toronto Globe and Mail and seven other newspapers. I expected to do it for a year or two. Now, I have penned The Doctor Game column 52 weeks of every year for 38 years.

Clark Davey, editor at The Globe and Mail, told me when I wrote the first column, "Your life will never be the same again". He was right! Shortly thereafter, another editor remarked, "It's the job of a journalist to make people think". He should have added "It can also make them mad as hell, and sometimes get you fired or nearly killed".

As the years unfolded I learned as a journalist that hypocrisy and outright lies can be a part of major humanitarian organizations. In 1979 in my column I initiated a campaign to legalize heroin to ease the agony of terminal cancer patients, many of whom die in agony. Heroin had been a legal painkiller for 90 years in England and I thought this was a humanitarian endeavor. But one health organization accused me of being "a headline seeking journalist" and know-nothing. Others claimed morphine to be equal in effectiveness to heroin, an outright lie. Still others claimed "morphine worked most of the time", but had no suggestion of what to use if it didn't. In 1984, after a huge battle in which I had the financial and moral support of readers, heroin was legalized for pain control.

But the war was lost due to bureaucratic red tape. It became an unforgiveable medical tragedy that should never have happened. Heroin for the dying is not available. As I later wrote in The Globe and Mail, "The problems of our society are generated by supposedly intelligent people who are largely fools". I haven't changed my mind when I witness the current thinking surrounding similar social issues in our society

Over the years research for my column taught me the tragedy of this continent's number one killer, heart attack. So currently, I'm involved in an effort to rid this country of its cause. But my thoughts on this matter date back many years. An economist once remarked that, "If you keep going to hell you'll eventually get there". Today millions of people are on their way to medical disaster because, unlike religion, there's no loving God in medicine to forgive past sins. In effect, there are two kinds of diseases, those we get, and those we make. It's the ones we make, the deadly trio of obesity, type 2 diabetes and cardiovascular disease that take a terrible toll and will eventually bankrupt our health care system.

Yet anyone could have seen the clouds gathering. During the Korean War post-mortem examinations revealed that 77 percent of U.S. soldiers with an average age of 22 had significant coronary heart disease. One percent of the enemy had it! Now heart disease continues to be the major cause of illness and death. It's also shocking that every 40 seconds a new case of diabetes is diagnosed in North America. Obviously we are doing something wrong. Or as Pogo in the comic strip remarked, "We have identified the enemy and the enemy is us".

So what is it that is causing "the deadly trio" to ravage our population? The main culprit is the over-abundance of calories causing weight gain, abetted by a misconception of how to treat its prime complication, atherosclerosis. For instance, during a recent speaking tour I talked to several thousand readers who convinced me that big pharma has brain-washed both doctors and the public into believing that cholesterol-lowering drugs are the be-all-and-end-all to prevent coronary attack, in spite of their many side-effects.

This attitude reminds me of the old expression, "It's not what you don't know that gets you into trouble. It's the things you know for sure that ain't so". Today, cardiologists and others refuse to accept that Medi-C Plus™, a powder with a high concentration of vitamin C and lysine can both prevent and reverse atherosclerosis in coronary and other arteries. It's a revolutionary finding, based on scientific fact that should have hit the head-lines of every newspaper in the world.

My philosophy about medical treatment has changed dramat-ically over the years, particularly after interviews with Dr Linus Pauling. He and other researchers made it increasingly appar-ent that doctors are over-drugging patients with a vast array of questionable and dangerous prescription medication. Evolution did not plan for this chemical abuse and its harmful effects on kidneys, liver and other organs. This is why my recent columns stress that prescription drugs kill, natural remedies don't.

It's been said that desperate diseases require desperate cures. So I've reached another conclusion. If I had the power to improve the nation's health I'd prohibit daily TV commercials that tell us something is wrong with us. I'd do this because Madison Avenue advertising is triggering false hopes and injuring health. We've reached a point where a well person is someone who hasn't been seen by enough doctors, or had a battery of tests done. Then we could dump half of the pills in the trash.

I also believe that, in moderation, alcohol may be the best medicine ever invented. This is why I wrote, only half in jest, that a pub in every hospital would ease more suffering than most other treatments. Lastly, I'm convinced that, although humour once got me fired from some newspapers, if you lose your sense of humour you lose everything. This is why I end this book with the "Fractured Male Organ", a little Ha Ha for the reader.

Remember any medical advice in this book is my personal opinion and you must consult your own doctor.

For more information see the web site www.docgiff.com
For comments info@docgiff.com

W. Gifford-Jones, MD

Chapter 1 - *Column 1*

Prescription Drugs Kill – Natural Remedies Rarely

Why is this patient taking a prescription medication when a natural drug would be just as effective? It's a question I ask more and more, the longer I practice medicine. There's no question that diabetes patients need insulin, and prescription drugs improve the quality of life for many people. But many drug complications could be avoided if doctors first considered natural remedies.

For instance, millions of North Americans are taking potentially dangerous medication to treat digestive problems. A report in the *Archives of Internal Medicine* states that drugs such as Nexium®, Prevacid® and Pantoloc® (proton-pump inhibitors known as PPIs) are being inappropriately prescribed over 50 percent of the time. The problem is that doctors prescribe PPIs for problems such as gastritis when less powerful drugs could be effective.

A Boston study showed that patients taking PPIs had a 74 percent greater risk of developing *Clostridium difficile*, a serious bowel infection that can cause up to 40 bowel movements a day.

There is a safer, more natural way to treat digestive problems and it's amazing there's so little information about it. In 1998, The New England Journal of Medicine reported that one gram of mastic, a resin-based plant taken daily for two weeks, can quickly cure peptic ulcers and decrease the risk of stomach cancer.

Today, millions of people are on cholesterol-lowering drugs (CLDs). They and their doctors are convinced that CLDs de-

2 *What I Learned as a Medical Journalist*

crease the risk of coronary attack. Studies do show these drugs reduce this risk but at a price of complications.

One problem is that CLDs decrease the amount of coenzyme Q10 in the heart muscle by as much as 40 percent. CoQ10 provides energy to the heart just as gasoline does to the car. Robbing the heart of CoQ10 may be setting people up for heart failure later in life. But how many doctors and pharmaceutical companies stress the need for CoQ10 to patients taking CLDs?

Millions of North Americans are also being treated for hypertension with prescription drugs. But patients with a mild increase in blood pressure can sometimes circumvent these drugs if doctors first advised an increase in magnesium. This mineral, along with calcium and potassium, relaxes blood vessels.

Studies show that most North Americans are magnesium deficient. This important mineral is necessary for the electrical conduction system of the heart. Patients who take prescription drugs to restore the heart's normal rhythm might be able to sidestep them if doctors first suggested the use of magnesium tablets.

Untold numbers of people are suffering from arthritis and neuromuscular problems. All too often, they're reaching for over-the-counter painkillers such as non-steroidal anti-inflammatory drugs, e.g. aspirin, Advil®, naproxen and others. But these painkillers cause the death of 25,000 North Americans every year due to gastrointestinal bleeding. Chronic use can also cause kidney damage. It makes more sense to use a safe, natural, pain-relieving cream, such as Celadrin, before resorting to these painkillers.

Low Intensity Laser Therapy, available in many chiropractic offices, can often ease the pain of arthritis, back pain, tendonitis and other joint problems. See the web site www.docgiff.com to learn how this therapy saved me from major surgery.

Some patients require a combination of natural and prescription drugs. For instance, antibiotics are often needed to cure a urinary infection. But many patients could save themselves from a second course of antibiotics by taking cranberry pills on a daily basis. For years, the curative power of cranberry juice was believed to be an old wives' tale. However, Harvard researchers proved that it prevents bacteria from sticking to the wall of the urinary bladder, often preventing another infection and the risk of an adverse antibiotic reaction.

A prime principle of medicine has always been, "First, do no harm". Over the years, this edict has become more and more difficult to ensure. Medicines that were vaunted to be medical breakthroughs are found several years later to cause catastrophic disease.

Of course, we need prescription drugs. But the blunt fact is that they can kill or cause serious complications. Natural remedies rarely do. So good sense dictates that they should be tried first before using the latest wonder drug.

Chapter 1 - *Column 2*

So Health Canada, Where are all the Dead Bodies?

Do you know that every day, 290 North American citizens are killed by prescription drugs? To kill that same number of people, a jumbo jet would have to crash every day. So why are natural remedies being removed from health food stores while drugs that kill remain available?

Dr. Zoltan Rona, an expert on natural remedies, recently told me that, "Health Canada has been raiding health food stores, terrorizing proprietors and confiscating natural food supplements." He asked, "Could you help to stop it?"

Rona described a New York Times report that the government's primary suspect in 542 deaths was Pradaxa®, a blood thinning agent. Moreover, when this drug causes bleeding there is no antidote to stop it. Yet Health Canada has done nothing to remove Pradaxa® from the market. However, it has removed a competitor, the soy-derived enzyme Nattokinase. This is a safe, effective, natural, blood thinner that has not harmed anyone and has been used for centuries in Japan.

While researching this column, I interviewed several authorities who were concerned that other natural remedies are no longer available. I also discovered a most disturbing fact. In Germany, a doctor's prescription is now required to obtain vitamin C! A red light flashed as I've recently reported that Medi-C Plus™, a powder that contains a high concentration of vitamin

C and lysine, can prevent and reverse coronary heart disease.

Germans now pay $45.00 for 90 tablets of 500 milligrams of vitamin C. Since I take several thousand milligrams of vitamin C in Medi-C Plus™ daily, this asinine ruling would cost me $3,600 annually for C!

This shows how far governments will go to control natural remedies. It's sheer, unadulterated madness since there is no known toxic amount of vitamin C. For instance, research has proven that it is safe to give several hundred thousand milligrams of vitamin C, day after day intravenously, to fight infection.

Today, many people are taking Sytrinol®, a natural remedy consisting of citrus and palm fruit extract which decreases total and bad cholesterol, decreases triglycerides and increases good cholesterol. For the moment, it's still available and there's no scientific reason it should be removed. But if that happens, patients will be forced to switch to cholesterol-lowering drugs (CLDs) whose safety record leaves much to be desired.

Alan Cassels, a drug policy researcher at the University of Victoria, says that, "cholesterol-lowering drugs are not worth the risk and history will regard CLDs as an unmitigated scandal in medicine". Readers know I share this view. But hell will freeze over before Health Canada raises an alarm and closes the door on these multi-billion dollar, risky products. Money and high paid lobbyists have won the day in Ottawa and Washington.

Many North Americans are taking products such as BioSil® to prevent osteoporosis (fragile bones). This natural product safely deposits calcium and phosphate into bone where they belong, rather than into arteries where they cause trouble. It's even more effective if used along with vitamin D3 which helps to absorb calcium from the bowel and vitamin K2 that deposits calcium and phosphate into bone. Will these people be forced to take drugs such as *Fosamax®* and *Actonel®* that have been associated with unusual fractures and degeneration of the jaw bone?

If government bureaucrats are honestly interested in the welfare of medical consumers, the best way for them to make an assessment is to examine records of the dead bodies. Data collected from 57 U.S. Poison Control Centers showed that in 2010, there were no deaths from the use of vitamin and herbal supplements – this in spite of the fact that there were 60 billion doses of nutritional supplements taken!

So where will these amateur forensic bureaucrats find the dead bodies? It doesn't require a long tedious search. *The Journal of the American Medical Association* claims that there are 60,000 deaths from drug use in the U.S. and 10,000 in Canada every year. Now it's the 4th leading cause of death after cancer, heart disease, and stroke.

The point is prescription drugs can kill, natural remedies never. It's time that Health Canada learned this message.

Chapter 2 - *Column 1*

Don't Become a Diabetic Statistic

When a man applied for a job at the railway station he was asked, "Suppose you saw a train coming from the east at 100 miles an hour. Then noticed a train coming from the west at 100 mph. The trains are both on the same track and just a quarter of a mile apart. What would you do?" The man replied, "I'd run and get my brother". "Why would you ever do that at such a critical time?" he was asked. The man replied, "Because my brother's never seen a train wreck".

Today, diabetes and its complications make a perfect medical train wreck. According to The World Health Organization, a new diabetic is diagnosed in North America every 40 seconds. Can you imagine the hue and cry if there were a new case of SARS or measles every 40 seconds?

The figures are appalling. Fifty years ago, 90 percent of diabetes was the result of inheriting bad genes (Type 1 diabetes). Now, 90 percent is due to obesity (Type 2)! Five percent of North Americans are diabetic. One child in five born today will become a diabetic. The dollars required to care for these patients is mind-boggling, eventually decimating our health care system. So can you decrease the risk of becoming a diabetes statistic?

First, everyone must get "scared as hell" about gaining weight. Excess weight not only sets the stage for diabetes, it also triggers a series of other health problems. For instance, heart disease is listed as the number one killer. But often it's sheer fat that's killing them.

Next, be "scared as hell" about packaged foods. Since most of us are no longer "down on the farm", packaged foods have now become a way of life. So, develop the habit of never buying packaged food without looking at the label. You will be surprised at the number of calories present per serving. Until everyone starts thinking calories, the battle of the bulge will never be won. Most people need approximately 1,800 calories a day.

Also, get "scared as hell" about other calories. For example, the 14 teaspoons of sugar present in a piece of cherry pie. I'm sure readers would conclude that I needed a psychiatrist if I poured eight teaspoons of sugar into a glass of water. But this is the amount kids have been drinking for years in one soft drink. And since many morning cereals contain 50 percent sugar, I tell my grandchildren it's safer to eat the box!

It's naive to expect that the epidemic of Type 2 diabetes will suddenly end. That would require a famine, a major public health assault on obesity or millions of people getting "scared as hell". I don't see this happening.

The great tragedy is that too many people look on diabetes simply as a problem with an excessive amount of blood sugar. They fail to realize the primary cause is narrowed atherosclerotic arteries that gradually choke off blood supply to vital organs.

The most appalling example of tragedy is what is happening to aboriginal patients in Manitoba. Because of diabetes and reduced blood supply to the legs, a high percentage of leg amputations are performed on aboriginals!

But looking at other diabetes patients in North America, diminished blood flow makes them 25 times more prone to blindness and 17 times more likely to be attached to renal dialysis machines due to destroyed kidneys.

Narrowed arteries in diabetes patients also carry less blood to the heart's muscle. This explains why 50 percent of them die of coronary attack.

Aging is also responsible for narrowed atherosclerotic arteries. But Dr. Sydney Bush, a British researcher, has shown that diabetes patients and the rest of us, can restore normal blood flow by taking high concentrations of vitamin C and lysine. It's recently become available as a powder called Medi-C Plus™ and is available in health food stores.

Unfortunately, neither diabetes patients nor others are aware of Medi-C Plus™ since its proven results have gone unrecognized by doctors.

Chapter 2 - *Column 2*

Why your Child May Die before You

What is the greatest tragedy that can befall parents? It's that a child will die before they do. It's tragic when this happens and we will see it more often.

Many years ago, I attended a service in Westminster Abbey in London, England. I can't recall the sermon. But I do remember seeing chubby choir boys. I realized then how obesity was starting to affect children. Since that time, several studies have shown the growing extent of childhood obesity.

One study in Nova Scotia involved 5,517 Grade Five students in 291 public schools. Of these students, 32.9 percent were overweight and 9.9 percent obese. One in 10 is a frightening figure.

We don't need any more reports of what common sense should tell everyone. Students were less obese when schools had regular physical education classes. Several asinine reasons are given for why they no longer exist. Some school boards in low income areas claim to have no funds to purchase recreation and gymnastic equipment or no time for such activity.

But preventive measures against obesity don't all require money and time. We know that children of families who eat together regularly are less likely to be overweight or obese. Dining together prevents children from eating in front of the television. Researchers found that T.V. munching often leads to what they called "mindless eating", with increased caloric intake. We've all seen that scenario.

If a child is driven to school instead of walking this routine adds pounds. So do soft drinks if they're available at school. And if the household income is under $60,000 the study shows there's a greater chance a child will be overweight.

The problem that should worry parents and society is that obese children are starting to show medical problems which used to be seen primarily in adults. Dr. Noel Merz, a Los Angeles cardiologist, reported this trend at a meeting of The American College of Cardiology.

Dr. Merz pointed out that today's children are now exposed to a diet high in calories. She stated further that, "Only in North America can we manufacture a reduced-fat Oreo® cookie that actually has more fat than the original one!" Today, doctors are seeing fatty degeneration of the liver in teenagers.

Another California study showed that 37 percent of Latino children had elevated blood cholesterol and 14 percent suffered from rising blood pressure.

This portends big trouble down the road. There's already shocking physical evidence of what's happening. Dr. Jacques Bart, another California researcher, reported that ultrasound of carotid arteries showed thickened atherosclerotic walls in 11 percent of adolescents studied. This finding would normally be seen only in adults.

The presence of thickened carotid arteries also means thickened atherosclerotic coronary arteries. The terrible truth is that obese children are developing adult diseases early in life. And it does not take deep thinking to predict that many will succumb before their parents to diabetes, heart attack and stroke.

It should be top priority for health authorities to find funding for schools in low income areas to encourage participation in sports. It makes no sense to penny-pinch on schoolyard equipment and then spend millions later treating fatal diseases that should never happen.

But in the final analysis, it's parents that must become pro-active in school matters. Remember, it's your child who is in danger. I know one group of parents in Toronto who recently raised $20,000 for outdoor school equipment.

There's no secret to preventing clogged arteries in children. It's common sense that children should start using their legs and stop mindless munching in front of TV. Parents should toss out packaged foods loaded with sugar and salt. And how many kitchens have a calorie book to show how calories mount up? Or a bathroom scale to monitor weight? It's biologically unnatural for children to die before their parents, especially from prevent-able causes. Regrettably, it will happen.

Chapter 2 - *Column 3*

Styrofoam™ Popcorn and How to Trick a Bartender

Why do people eat more than they should? You say you've heard all the reasons? But I bet you're dead wrong. Why? Because a report in *The Nutrition Action Health Letter* is written by a marketing expert, not a doctor. As well, there's a way to get rid of unwelcome dinner guests and trick a bartender.

Brian Wansink, Professor of Marketing at Cornell University, in Ithaca, New York, directs the Food and Brand Lab. He asks people, "When was the last time you ate to the point of regretting it?" He follows that with, "Why did you do it?" He receives the usual answers, "It was a tough day" or "I was depressed". But most replied they were hungry and the food looked good.

But Wansink decided to find out what happens if the person isn't hungry and the food terrible. In one experiment, researchers gave free popcorn to theatre-goers who had had dinner 20 minutes earlier. The popcorn was five days old and tasted like Styrofoam™. It was given in medium or large bags. Researchers discovered that even people, who were not hungry and given lousy food, ate 34 percent more popcorn from the larger bag.

Several external cues make us overeat. We can all say, "We're smart and we can use our brain to overcome such cues." But even intelligent people fail the test due to what Wansink calls, "Mindless Eating" and "The Intelligence Trap".

Wansink told highly motivated, intelligent students, "If I give you a big bowl, you will eat more than from a slightly smaller bowl." He then showed them lectures on how to avoid this trap and the students subsequently left for a holiday vacation.

After they returned, he invited them to a Super Bowl party at a sports bar. One room had enormous bowls of Chex® Mix snacks while another identical room had slightly smaller bowls of Chex® Mix. Wansink discovered that those serving themselves from the larger bowl consumed 53 percent more food. All the earlier lectures had no effect, even though it was the same food as shown in the videos.

So you want to get more scotch for your money from a bartender? It's quite easy. Wansink told bartenders with six years' experience to put the same amount of alcohol into either short, wide glasses or high, thin ones. But even with their experience, they poured 20 percent more alcohol into the short wide glasses.

Why does this happen? Wansink says that smart people believe they're smarter than the bowl or the glass even if they're a Harvard graduate.

You own an Italian restaurant and want to sell more pasta? Just change the name from "Italian Pasta" to "Succulent Tuscany Pasta". This increases sales by 27 percent. Patrons also rate the restaurant better and the chef more competent. You can get the same increase by changing "chocolate cake" to "Belgium Black Forest Cake". Names can make you eat more.

So can expectation. If you have guests who drink too much of your good wine and you want to get rid of them, try this restaurant experiment. Wansink bought cheap $2.00 cabernet wine and soaked off the labels. He replaced them with labels from California and North Dakota. (North Dakota doesn't even make wine!).

Those who drank "California wine" rated the restaurant better and made reservations to return. The "North Dakota wine" poisoned the entire meal. These participants rated the food as poor, left early and made no further reservations.

So what does work to fight obesity? Wansink advises the use of smaller bowls. He does not believe that education makes a difference. Make sure the first thing seen on the table is healthier food. And cover the clear window of the ice cream freezer with butcher paper to decrease the urge for ice cream.

If you buy in bulk, break it down into small packages to decrease the amount you eat. When candy is in small mini-packs, 70 percent of people will eat less.

I can hardly wait to ask the next bartender to put my drink in a short, wide glass.

Chapter 3 - *Column 1*

PGX® Fibre Fights Obesity

What's the best way to fight the battle of the bulge? It's not by buying books or starting fad diets that rarely work. Rather, there's a natural way to lose weight by adding PGX® fibre to the daily menu. It's shocking that most people are unaware of the huge role fibre plays in combating obesity.

Several years ago, I wrote about a simple method to determine if patients were taking sufficient fibre by examining their stools. If stools failed to float, or were not as soft as toothpaste, they were lacking fibre. Some readers accused me of giving them a stiff neck by trying to find out!

Most North Americans consume about 15 grams of fibre daily. That is less than half the amount they need which is 35 grams. The result is people often have stools as hard as rocks, suffer from constipation, hemorrhoids, irritable bowel syndrome, and diverticulosis (small hernias of the large bowel). But this lack of fibre also triggers obesity with all its lethal complications, diabetes, hypertension, heart attack and stroke.

Recently, the National Institutes of Health reported on a *Diet and Health Study*. This research revealed a link between dietary fibre and a reduced risk from cardiovascular, infectious and respiratory disease, as well as decreased risk of death from any cause.

But how does fibre prevent so many diverse problems? The secret is "filling volume" – fibre makes the stomach feel full and diminishes the hunger reflex. For instance, no one with an ounce of good sense would add eight teaspoons of sugar to a glass of water and drink it. But for years, children and others have been drinking cans of cola with that same amount of sugar. A cola drink adds to obesity as it has loads of calories and no filling volume. Contrast this to eating an apple that contains fibre. It's rare that anyone asks for a second one, because apples have filling volume.

So why don't people eat more fibre? Simply put – it doesn't taste as good as fancy desserts, ice cream and other sweets. The result is that too many people bypass a high fibre breakfast, whole wheat bread and other high fibre foods.

PGX® (PolyGlycopleX) is a super fibre that helps to supplement inadequate fibre intake. It's been reported in several international journals and is a complex of natural polysaccharides. Gram for gram these provide more fibre punch than any other fibres.

When PGX® softgels are swallowed with a glass of water, they expand because of their great ability to absorb many times their weight in water. This tells the brain that the stomach is full, with no need for second helpings of food.

PGX® also combats the effect of today's sugary diet with its yo-yo effect on blood sugar levels, often the forerunner of Type 2 diabetes. PGX® decreases this risk by slowing digestion of food. This places less stress on the hormone insulin, which regulates blood sugar, resulting in more stable levels.

Studies show PGX® decreases cholesterol by 17 percent and also helps to lower blood triglycerides. With its high fibre content, it fights constipation by absorbing large amounts of water.

The dose of PGX® is one to two softgels before meals along with a glass of water. This creates the same result as three bowls of oatmeal! The dose can be gradually increased over several days. Taking too much initially can cause bloating or loose stools.

Patients should take any medication one hour before PGX® or two to three hours afterwards. PGX® can slow the absorption of drugs, so always check with your doctor before taking it with any medication.

Some nutrition authorities now consider PGX® to be the "Holy Grail" in treating obesity. But always remember that no magic potion will create weight loss unless it is also associated with a total commitment to stop a faulty lifestyle. So get off the couch, follow a sound diet, buy a scale and watch calories.

PGX is available at most health food stores.

Chapter 3 - *Column 2*

PGX® Fights Constipation, Cholesterol and Obesity

W. C. Fields, the comedian with the bulbous, red, alcoholic nose, when asked if he would like a glass of water always replied, "Water is for flowing under bridges". But Fields didn't know about "The Ultimate Volumetrics Diet" or PGX®.

Dr. Barbara Rolls, Professor of Nutritional Sciences at Penn State University in Pennsylvania, reports in the publication *"Nutrition Action"* that, when she was studying the effects of fats, carbohydrates and proteins in food intake, she had a "Eureka" moment. People, she concluded, were not regulating their calories. Rather, they were eating the same weight or volume of food.

Her next "Eureka" moment was the observation that it's possible to eat a large volume of food and still lose weight if the large portions are low in calories.

W.C. Fields didn't know the secret is the amount of water in food. This doesn't mean you have to pour water into your favourite meal. Rather, it means adding vegetables to a casserole and dinner plate because vegetables are mostly water. So you end up with a mouthful of heavier food per bite, but with fewer calories.

Dr. Rolls says it's possible to chew on low density celery, salad greens, tomato, apples and whole wheat spaghetti, without gaining excessive weight. But it's easy to add pounds with high density calorie foods such as carrot cake, brownies, chocolate chips and peanut butter.

But trying to sort out the good foods from the bad gets complicated when Dr. Rolls suggests calculating the caloric density of foods by dividing calories by weight in grams. It's a scientific approach, but hell will freeze over before anyone does it.

A less complicated routine, suggested by Dr. Rolls, is having a low calorie, dense soup, salad or an apple at the start of a meal. These fill up the stomach, decreasing the hunger reflex.

I have also believed that the best way to tame the hunger reflex is by a high fibre diet. Most North Americans consume 15 grams of fibre daily, but they need 35. This means many people have stools as hard as rocks, and suffer from constipation and obesity.

The "Eureka" moment that everyone should experience is the simple, indisputable fact that fibre has what's called "filling volume" which tells the brain the stomach is full.

Of course, good sense indicates it's prudent to use dietary means and exercise to combat obesity. But the wrong foods usually win out, resulting in the current epidemic of obesity and diabetes.

So if you're losing the battle of the bulge, what else can you do? PGX® is a complex of natural polysaccharides, and gram for gram provides greater filling volume than other fibres. The softgels or granules, when swallowed with meals, expand because of their great ability to absorb many times their weight in water, thus decreasing the hunger reflex.

There's another important function. High spikes in blood sugar create a yo-yo effect and increase the risk of Type 2 diabetes. PGX, by slowing the digestion of food, moderates blood sugar levels. This lowers what's called, the glycemic index (GI) and decreases the risk of type 2 diabetes. Studies also show that overweight and obese people with a low GI tend to lose weight. PGX® also decreases blood cholesterol levels by 17 percent.

The minimum dose of PGX® is three softgels or 2.5 grams of granules daily before meals with a glass of water or added to moist foods. This creates the same effect as three bowls of oatmeal.

However, some people feel full on less. If this is the case, you can use a gradual approach by adding one or two softgels or one gram of the PGX® granules to meals throughout the day.

So I'd agree with Dr Rolls – there's more benefit to water than merely flowing under bridges. And for losing weight, there's nothing gram for gram that's better than a high fibre diet. That's why PGX® has been called the "Holy Grail" in the treatment of obesity.

PGX® is available in most health food stores.

Chapter 4 - *Column 1*

The "Ain't So's" about Cholesterol

Why are people so misinformed about cholesterol when so much has been published about it? After all, cholesterol has become a household name. It's even hard to go to a social gathering without someone mentioning this fatty substance and their own cholesterol level. But as one wise sage remarked, "It's not the things you don't know that gets you into trouble. It's the things you know for sure that ain't so". So what ain't so about cholesterol?

It ain't so, for instance, that the only cause of coronary artery disease is cholesterol. Life is not that simple and it's totally unrealistic to believe that one risk factor sends so many people to the great beyond. Rather, Mathew's Law is the culprit. It states that "it's the sum total of several factors such as obesity, diabetes, hypertension, lack of exercise, smoking, advancing age and inadequate fibre in the diet that ends so many lives."

It ain't so that cholesterol is the devil it's made out to be. How many people know that cholesterol is a necessary part of every cell in the body? Cholesterol is required for the absorption of fats, and digestive juices, and there would be no loving without cholesterol as it is needed to produce sex hormones! We would all die without cholesterol. And how many are aware that some studies show cholesterol-lowering drugs (CLDs) increase the risk of violent death, suicide, short term memory loss and some cancers?

It ain't so that cholesterol numbers determine whether or not you have a heart attack. Cholesterol levels of men living in Edinburgh, Scotland and Stockholm, Sweden, are identical. But the coronary death rate is three times greater in Scots. Maybe they don't eat as many veggies. Or drink too much of their own Scotch! Similarly, ethnic Japanese living in Japan and California have comparable blood cholesterol levels, but those in California have more coronary disease. Is this because of a change in diet or stress from driving their highways? No one really knows the answer to these questions.

It ain't so that low levels of blood cholesterol prevent atherosclerosis and heart attack. One of the world's most famous Texas heart surgeons reported years ago that 30 percent of patients who had a coronary bypass operation had normal blood cholesterol levels.

It ain't so that the only way our bodies obtain cholesterol is by the food we eat. Most patients are amazed to hear the liver produces 80 to 90 percent of the cholesterol in our bodies. You can't change the spots on a leopard and it's hard to change the genetically-controlled metabolism of the liver. Dietary changes help, but it requires a drastic change in food consumption to significantly reduce blood cholesterol.

It ain't so that the more cholesterol we eat the more cholesterol is in the blood. The production of cholesterol by the liver acts much like the thermostat that controls the temperature of our homes. Studies show that the more cholesterol consumed, the less the liver produces. Conversely, if the diet is low in cholesterol the reverse is true, and the liver manufactures more cholesterol.

Here's a big "Ain't so." It's not simply medical science that convinces people to take cholesterol-lowering drugs and other medication. I often write this column on Lake Canandaigua in upper state New York, so I keep my eye on U.S. health matters. It was recently reported by the health insurance company Excellus Blue Cross Blue Shield that in 2007, in upper state N.Y. alone, $241,530,000 was spent on just one cholesterol drug, Lipitor®! Another $103,580,000 on Prevacid® to ease stomach problems and $74,360,000 on Effexor® for depression. The point is, "Thars money in them thar drugs."

I find it hard to believe that in one small corner of the U.S. so many people are suffering from high cholesterol levels, stomach and nervous problems, to name just a few. We have more than a sick economy these days. We have a population that's been programmed to illness. A population that now believes that the road to health is paved with pills, pills and more pills. And it means we have a terribly ill society that keeps pharmaceutical companies flourishing.

Chapter 4 - *Column 2*

Should You Fly over that Big Gaping Hole?

A picture is often worth a thousand words. One recently caught my eye. The picture shows a small plane circling a huge active volcano. A passenger says, "Let's take a closer look at the volcanic crater". The pilot replies, "We can't, it's not worth the risk".

Dr. Jim Wright is Director of The Therapeutic Initiative. It's a British Columbia organization that aids doctors in evaluating drugs. It concluded that cholesterol-lowering drugs may be doing more harm than good in the attempt to prevent heart attack.

After studying five clinical trials of CLDs, Dr. Wright reported that the drugs only decreased the risk of heart attack and stroke by a mere 1.4 per cent over a three-to-five year period.

He adds that, "If I were a physician, I would have to treat 71 people with CLDs for one to benefit". Moreover, he expressed concern that cholesterol-lowering drugs may have increased other health problems such as cancer and psychiatric troubles.

This is not the first time researchers have questioned the use of cholesterol-lowering drugs. In 1990, the *British Medical Journal* published a study involving 25,000 men. Half of these men had lowered their blood cholesterol primarily with drugs. The result? The men using drug therapy had 28 fewer heart attacks than the other group without this medication. But the benefit was offset by 29 additional violent deaths such as accidents, suicides and homicides.

Later that year, the National Heart, Lung and Blood Institute reviewed all the data on cholesterol blood levels and mortality rates. They reported their findings in the journal *Circulation* (a publication of the American Heart Association), after analyzing 19 studies. Their findings showed that high blood cholesterol levels were associated with an increased risk of heart disease, at least in men. But low blood cholesterol levels, in both men and women, showed a 40 per cent greater risk of death from non-cardiac causes such as violent death, lung disease and some cancers. In an editorial accompanying this report, Dr. Stephen Hulley, of the University of California at San Francisco, strongly recommended that CLDs should not be used except in patients who already showed signs of heart disease.

Then in July 1992, the *Archives of Internal Medicine* reported on a study involving 351,000 men. This showed that low cholesterol levels were associated with increased risk of hemorrhagic stroke, liver disease, pancreatic cancer, digestive disease, cirrhosis of the liver and alcoholism.

For years, I have questioned the widespread use of cholesterol-lowering drugs. There is no doubt that the general consensus among doctors is that CLDs save lives. So my doubts are not shared by many others.

So why am I so reluctant to climb aboard this bandwagon that touts the cardiovascular benefits of CLDs? For one thing, I don't believe you can totally ignore the studies that show adverse side effects. After all, it's well known CLDs can damage liver and kidneys and that patients have died from their use. That's a big price to pay.

I'm also a great believer in the use of common sense. Today, some authorities claim it's important to push blood cholesterol levels even lower using CLDs. In effect, they are saying that if low cholesterol is good for you, an even lower one is better. This reasoning worries me. Cholesterol is an essential nutrient for repairing cell membranes that manufacture vitamin D and produce hormones, such as estrogen and testosterone.

The economics of CLDs also concerns me. Money drives many things and it's had a huge impact on CLDs. Massive amounts of money are spent on their promotion because great profit is made from the sale of CLDs. Moreover, much of the research has been paid for by the pharmaceutical industry and he who pays the piper often calls the tune.

All this has created a nation of cholesterol phobiacs. People talk about the reduction of cholesterol numbers as if they were searching for the Holy Grail.

Since I'm not related to the Almighty, I may be terribly wrong. But I believe history will show that the level of blood cholesterol is not the huge culprit it's made out to be.

New Report on Risk of Cholesterol Drugs

How will history judge me for questioning the benefits of cholesterol-lowering drugs (CLDs)? I'll never know. But a report in the *British Medical Journal* that studied 226,000 people taking CLDs now says that muscle and back pain may be more frequent than originally believed. For instance, muscle pain and weakness occurred in up to one-third of patients. Moderate or severe muscle pain in 100 to 300 women.

Severe muscle pain is a worrying symptom as it may be the prelude to rhabdomyolysis. This is a life-threatening condition where large amounts of muscle tissue are destroyed causing kidney failure. The complication occurs in about one in 10,000 patients. So if muscle pain develops while taking a cholesterol-lowering drug, it should be reported immediately to the doctor.

The journal *Lancet* reports a 2010 study showing that one case of Type 2 diabetes occurs for every 255 people who take CLDs for four years. Other research has linked CLDs to cataracts, liver problems and mental confusion.

The most classic case of brain dysfunction involved Dr. Duane Graveline, a physician and NASA astronaut. During a routine checkup, NASA physicians found that Dr. Graveline had an elevated blood cholesterol. Doctors prescribed Lipitor® to correct this problem. Several months later, Graveline arrived home and did not know where he was and could not recognize his family. NASA physicians refused to believe that his amnesia was related to Lipitor®, but they discontinued the drug. Graveline gradually recovered his senses.

Later, NASA doctors prescribed half the dose of Lipitor® and after several months, Graveline's problem recurred. Finally, doctors admitted that Lipitor® was associated with the development of transient global amnesia. Since his retirement from NASA, Dr. Graveline has authored several books criticizing the use of CLDs.

Today, millions of people are taking CLDs. There is no evidence of an epidemic of transient global amnesia or other problems. So, at the moment, one can say they're "relatively" safe. But to conclude that the use of CLDs is a reasonable and responsible way to decrease cardiovascular disease, is in my opinion, questionable. Readers may wonder if I take CLDs since I have an elevated blood cholesterol. The answer is, "No" and several cardiologists say I'm making a bad mistake. They may be right. This does not imply that I play Russian Roulette with my life. But I'm skeptical of research that I believe exaggerates the benefits. Statistics can always be manipulated to show great results.

Besides, I'm not the only person who questions the use of CLDs. Dr. Vikas Sukhatme, Professor of Medicine at The Harvard Medical School, developed leg pain while taking a CLD. This prompted him to discover a gene called atrogen-1, which triggers the breakdown of proteins in muscle tissue. He also showed that the higher the dose, the greater the destruction of muscle tissue.

Another researcher, Dr. Annette Draeger, from the University of Berne, Switzerland, obtained biopsies of CLD patients complaining of muscle pain. Significant muscle injury was shown in 57 percent of these patients.

Other researchers are concerned that by lowering blood cholesterol, patients may be substituting one devil for another. For instance, in one study those taking CLDs had 22 fewer deaths from cardiovascular disease, but 24 more deaths from cancer. Hardly a good exchange!

But my prime reason for bypassing CLDs is that I believe Dr. Linus Pauling, two-time Nobel Prize winner, and Professor Sydney Bush, a distinguished British optometrist, are right. Pauling stressed that since humans, unlike animals, do not produce vitamin C, this causes atherosclerosis in coronary arteries and heart attack.

Dr. Bush proved Pauling right. Bush prescribed 6,000 milligrams of vitamin C to patients using contact lenses. He took photographs of their retinal arteries before starting vitamin C and then again, one year later. The second photographs showed that atherosclerosis was regressing. What happens in retinal arteries must also occur in coronary vessels.

So I'll take my chance with vitamin C. You can get the complete story on vitamin C and the amino acid lysine at www.medi-c.ca.

Chapter 4 - *Column 4*

Which Do You Prefer – Heart Attack or Diabetes?

Is it getting easier for patients to make the right health decision today, compared to 50 years ago? It should be, considering the huge advances in medical knowledge since that time. But unless you're blessed with the "Wisdom of Solomon", these advances may merely help you exchange one disease for another. Or, as one wise sage remarked, "Life would be easier if there were no 'buts'."

For instance, a study reported in the *Annals of Internal Medicine*, has depressing news for those taking cholesterol-lowering drugs (CLDs). Researchers studied thousands of middle-aged and older women for seven years who were taking CLDs. Their conclusion? Compared to those women who were not taking this medication, they were 50 percent more likely to develop diabetes. This is hardly what one would call a therapeutic home-run.

Another huge CLD study followed 150,000 women in their 50s, 60s and 70s for seven years. Again, this group was 48 percent more likely to develop diabetes than those not on this medication. Other earlier studies showed that men on CLDs were 12 percent more prone to develop this disease.

No one at the moment knows why CLDs are linked to the development of diabetes. We've known for years that they can cause liver, muscle and kidney problems. So it's not surprising that these drugs can also have an adverse effect on the metabolism of sugar.

Researchers concluded that, although patients faced an increased risk of diabetes when taking CLDs, the benefits far outweighed the risk. This is particularly true for people who have existing heart disease or have had a previous stroke. But I think one could debate this point.

The history of CLDs shows several other situations where patients exchange one devil for another. For instance, a major study called PROSPER (The Prospective Study of Pravastatin in the Elderly at Risk), revealed that those taking CLDs had 22 fewer deaths from cardiovascular disease. But this was offset by an increase of 24 deaths from cancer. Hardly a good exchange!

In other studies, high blood cholesterol was proven to be associated with increased risk of heart disease. But low cholesterol levels showed a greater risk of death from non-cardiac causes such as violent death, mental problems, liver and kidney disease, strokes and some cancers.

With advancing age, there is further cause for concern. After 50 years of age, an association has been shown between low cholesterol and an increased risk of death. Researchers at the University of Denmark reported that about 15 percent of those patients on CLDs over this age suffered nerve damage.

Dr. Annette Draeger, a researcher at the University of Switzerland, took muscle biopsies from 44 patients on CLDs who were complaining of muscle pain. Her results showed significant muscle damage in 57 percent of these biopsies.

It's not my intention to propose tossing away CLDs. Ninety-nine percent of physicians are convinced that these drugs are the "be-all-and-end-all" to prevent and treat cardiovascular problems. But I'm not convinced that is the case. I've stressed to patients and readers that I'm not related to the Almighty and could be 100 percent wrong.

I like to have an open mind on new medical advances, but not so open that my brain falls out. My brain tells me that something must be wrong when you have to accept the increased risk of diabetes and so many other potential problems when taking CLDs.

Today, we could prevent 90 percent of Type 2 diabetes simply by not being obese.

In addition, go to www.medi-c.ca to learn how Dr. Sydney Bush, a British researcher, has shown that large doses of vitamin C and lysine can reverse narrowing of coronary arteries and prevent heart attack. But cardiologists have closed minds when it comes to this research.

Chapter 4 - *Column 5*

Cholesterol-Lowering Drugs and Muscle Damage

Today, millions of people are taking cholesterol-lowering drugs (CLDs) known as statins. But how safe is this medication, particularly if patients are complaining of muscle pain? Doctors often reassure patients that if blood tests are normal, there's no need to worry. But a recent report in the *Canadian Medical Association Journal* shows that blood tests cannot guarantee that muscle injury is not occurring.

Dr. Annette Draeger of the University of Berne, Switzerland, and her colleagues obtained biopsy samples from 83 patients. Of the 44 patients complaining of muscle pain, 29 were taking a CLD and 15 had discontinued it for at least three weeks before biopsies were done. The study also included 19 patients who were taking a CLD and were free of muscle pain plus a control group who had never taken a CLD.

The researchers noted that in the past, muscle pain has normally been dismissed as a minor problem by both patients and doctors. But biopsies showed significant muscle injury in 57 percent of patients who complained of muscle pain. No muscle injury was present in those who had never taken a CLD.

Up to this point, the American College of Cardiology and the American Heart Association recommend that CLDs should be continued as long as blood levels of creatine phosphokinase, do not exceed 10 times the upper limit of normal. But only one patient who complained of muscle pain had an abnormal blood level of creatine phosphokinase.

This report shows that even those patients suffering from muscle pain and who have normal levels of creatine phosphokinase can still have muscle injury. In fact, muscle injury was seen in one of 19 patients on long-term CLDs who reported as having no muscle pain!

Dr. Draeger reported that the severity of muscle damage was not correlated to the type of CLD being used, the duration of use or the dosage. However, none of the patients were taking doses over 80 milligrams a day. So it's reasonable to speculate that if a low dose of CLD causes muscle injury, larger doses would cause increased muscle damage.

It was also admitted by Dr. Draeger that there could be even more muscle injury than was reported. All biopsies were taken from the vastus lateralis muscle in the thigh, regardless of where patients complained of pain. Again, it's logical to assume that if biopsies were done in the painful muscle, the rate of injury would be higher.

There was another interesting finding. Researchers were surprised to discover muscle injury in patients who had discontinued CLDs for a considerable time.

Dr. Richard H. Karas, of the Tufts New England Medical Center in Boston, said that these findings should not affect the clinical management of patients. Nor should they trigger alarm since the vast majority of patients taking CLDs do not suffer from muscle pain.

I don't find this statement overly reassuring. It's believed that about 10 to 15 percent of patients taking CLDs do complain of muscle pain, not an insignificant number considering the millions of patients taking these medications. And it now appears that blood tests are not a reliable way to determine if muscle injury is taking place.

We also know that, in rare situations, CLDs can cause rhabdomyolosis, a potentially fatal condition, in which large amounts of muscle tissue are destroyed causing kidney failure. It's a good reminder that patient's are not taking candy.

Today, a huge amount of information is available outlining the multiple benefits of CLDs. It's not the intention of this journalist to discount these potential advantages. Rather, I want to try and provide balance to what often appears to be an attempt to stress the benefits of CLDs and gloss over possible side effects.

I must add that the vast majority of doctors are convinced that the advantages of CLDs far outweigh these potential complications. So a decision about taking a CLD is totally dependent on the advice of your own doctor. After all, one in five of us will die of heart attack, so decisions of this type cannot be taken lightly.

"It Felt Like Somebody Had Put Lead on my Legs"

What sells newspapers? Bad news! And every morning I get tired of reading more of it. Good news is exceedingly hard to find, but there are exceptions. Medical publications continue to publish "good" news about cholesterol-lowering drugs (CLDs), that doctors should strive to get blood cholesterol lower and lower, that CLDs can be used to treat an increasing number of other medical problems. But since I'm more than a trifle skeptical about these drugs, it's refreshing to me to read the less than perfect news about CLDs from The Harvard Medical School.

Focus, Harvard's news bulletin, reports the medical problem of Dr. Vikas Sukhatme. He's Professor of Medicine at Harvard's Beth Israel Deaconess Medical Center in Boston, and like many of his patients and millions of others, he was taking a CLD to lower blood cholesterol.

A few years ago, Dr. Sukhatme noticed a dull pain in his back and legs. He said the pain was never debilitating, but "It felt like somebody had put lead on my legs". Knowing that CLDs could cause this symptom, he stopped the medication. It required nine months for the pain to subside.

Like any inquisitive physician, the doctor decided to test the drug again, and the pain returned. This spurred him to team up with a number of Harvard researchers in an effort to find the culprit.

By studying the effects of CLDs on muscle tissue, they discovered that a gene called atrogen-1, helped to trigger the breakdown of proteins in muscle tissue. Equally important, they found that the higher the dose, the greater the destruction of muscle tissue.

It's not the intention of this column to have everyone toss cholesterol drugs away. After all, millions of patients are taking this medication without apparent problems. But the news does raise questions.

We've known for several years that in extreme cases CLDs can cause rhabdomyolysis, a life-threatening condition. In these cases, the breakdown of muscle protein is so severe that it can result in kidney failure and death.

The big questions raised by this study are how much effect do CLDs have on muscles when patients complain of only mild leg pain and what is the effect on muscle tissue when physicians prescribe increasing doses of CLDs? At the moment no one can answer these questions.

I doubt that this information is going to hit the headlines. To question the value of CLDs is like denouncing Motherhood or apple pie. In this case, the tendency is to bury bad news.

I'm not the only doctor, however, to question the widespread use of CLDs. Dr. Jim Wright, Director of the Therapeutic Initiatives, an organization based at the University of British Columbia that evaluates drugs, believes that CLDs may be doing more harm than good in the attempt to prevent heart attack.

He reports that doctors would have to treat 71 patients with CLDs for one patient to benefit. And that these drugs have only decreased the risk of heart attack and stroke by a mere 1.4 percent over a three-to-five-year period.

Other researchers have shown that by using CLDs you may be substituting one devil for another. For example, in one study, those taking CLDs had 22 fewer deaths from cardiovascular disease. But this was offset by an increase of 24 deaths from cancer.

It has also been shown that over the age of 50, low cholesterol is associated with an increased risk of death. Researchers at the University of Denmark report that about15 percent of those over this age on CLDs suffer nerve damage.

Patients are always surprised when I tell them that cholesterol is a vital substance for bodily function that we all require to repair cell membranes and to manufacture vitamin D and sex hormones, both male and female. And that there's also a huge amount of cholesterol in brain tissue. This may explain why Duane Graveline, former NASA physician and astronaut, developed transient global amnesia when a CLD lowered his blood cholesterol.

Researchers are now trying to find ways of taming the gene atrogen-1 and decrease the risk of muscle injury. In the meantime, patients on CLDs who experience muscle pain should report this symptom to their doctor.

Chapter 4 - *Column 7*

How to Control Cholesterol Numbers by Natural Means

"Why don't you take my advice and start cholesterol-lowering drugs? You quote the expression in your column that 'he who treats himself has a fool for a patient.' And that's exactly what you're doing!" My cardiologist believes I'm making a huge mistake by saying no to cholesterol-lowering drugs.

I start the day with the right breakfast – not a doughnut and a cup of coffee. A report from The Mayo Clinic suggests oatmeal and oat bran. These soluble fibres reduce low density lipoprotein (LDL), the "bad" cholesterol, by binding with bile which contains cholesterol. So rather than being absorbed from the intestines, the cholesterol is excreted by the bowel.

You say you don't like oat bran. I don't either. But by adding a banana or other fruit, it's quite palatable. Remember, to live longer it's sometimes necessary to do what you don't like and you have to make a choice! I also add a half a spoonful of cinnamon to toast. Researchers at the Human Nutrition Research Center report that this amount of cinnamon decreases bad cholesterol by 20 percent.

Linus Pauling, two-time Noble Prize winner, advised me years ago to add vitamin C to my breakfast routine. So a flat teaspoon of Medi-C Plus™ powder (2,000 mg of vitamin C) goes into my orange juice. This amount increases the rate that cholesterol is removed from the blood. The body does this by converting cholesterol into bile acids that are then excreted from the bowel. I add the same amount of vitamin C to my evening meal.

Studies in the 1970s showed that Greenland Inuit had a lower rate of heart disease than other people living in Greenland at the same time. Later studies showed that the Inuit consumed less saturated fat and more omega-3 fatty acids found in fish, whale and seal meat.

Omega-3 fatty acids help to lower blood triglycerides. They are also beneficial to the heart by decreasing the risk of blood clots. That's why it's prudent to have three meals of fish every week. But you don't have to hunt for whale or seal meat. Sardines, mackerel, herring, salmon, albacore tuna and lake trout also have high levels of omega-3 fatty acids.

During the course of the day, while writing this column, I reach for nuts. Dr David Jenkins, Director of Clinical Nutrition at St. Michael's Hospital in Toronto, advises a handful of almonds every day. Jenkins studied 27 men and women with high cholesterol for three months. He reported that two handfuls of almonds daily reduced LDL by 9.4 percent. This amount also resulted in improvements in lowering total cholesterol and raising high density lipoproteins (HDL or the "good" cholesterol) that remove excess cholesterol from the blood. He says that a handful of almonds daily will decrease the risk of a cardiovascular event by 18 percent.

Almonds are also rich in polyunsaturated fatty acids which help to keep blood vessels soft and elastic. Remember, nuts are high in calories but if you eat sensibly, there's no need to gain weight on nuts.

Mayo Clinic researchers report that foods fortified by sterols and stanols can block the absorption of cholesterol. These substances found in plants and in products such as margarine and orange juice can lower LDL by 10 percent.

At the end of the day, I add a glass of red wine to boost HDL. It's also my treat for eating oat bran in the morning! Red wine decreases the formation of endothelium-1, a chemical that makes coronary arteries less likely to constrict causing angina. And by making blood platelets (part of the blood clotting system) slippery, there's less chance of a fatal blood clot. But only use this part of the prescription if you drink moderately.

Many other remedies are available for treating cholesterol, however, there's a limit to the number it's reasonable to try. After all, there's more to life than cholesterol.

As for my cardiologist, he may be right that I have a fool for a patient. But I prefer to take my chance on natural ways to control blood cholesterol. I think history will prove me right.

Remember this is my personal opinion and you must follow your own doctor's advice on this matter.

Chapter 4 - *Column 8*

Low Blood Cholesterol and Heart Failure

Today, the debate continues within various organizations as to when life begins. But for most people, there is no debate that life on this planet ends when the heart reaches its final beat. Now, researchers at Mount Sinai Hospital in New York City report that the final beat may be sooner for patients with "low" blood cholesterol. But should this fact be a surprise?

"How many times does your heart beat every 24 hours?" I've often asked this question and it invariably triggers a perplexed look as few know the answer. They're surprised when I tell them it's 100,000 times. For those who live to 70 years of age, the total number of beats in a lifetime is 2.52 billion. And, unlike most muscles, the heart never gets a holiday.

You can only beat a tired horse so long until it dies from exhaustion. The same situation applies to the heart's muscle which can become weak for several reasons. Patients following coronary attack may have a weakened heart due to the loss of muscle tissue. In other cases, the cause may be long-standing hypertension. Or damaged heart valves.

But the symptoms are always the same. Patients gradually become short of breath, fatigued, ankles swell and the effort to continue daily activities may be arduous.

For years, we have been told that high blood cholesterol was bad for the heart. In fact, some researchers claim that even those with normal blood cholesterol should endeavour to get it lower.

But now, studies show that lower blood cholesterol can be hazardous to your health. For instance, the PROSPER Study (The Prospective Study of Pravastatin in the Elderly at Risk), reveals that you can exchange one devil for another. It showed that low blood cholesterol was associated with 22 fewer deaths from cardiovascular disease, but there was an increase of 24 deaths from cancer, violent deaths, mental problems and kidney and liver disease. This is hardly a good exchange.

Another worrying finding for those over 50 years of age, showed low blood cholesterol associated with nerve damage in 15 percent of cases. Moreover, there was increased risk of death in those over this age.

The current study involved 2,500 patients suffering from heart failure. They were followed for three years to see if there was any relationship between the blood level of "bad" cholesterol (low density lipoprotein or LDL) and the overall risk of death.

Researchers concluded that those with decreased blood levels of LDL had a 68 percent increased risk of death compared to those with significantly higher levels. This is not the only study that reached this conclusion.

But why should low blood cholesterol be bad for you when for years, doctors have claimed it's the-be-all-and-end-all for a healthy heart? The answer is that cholesterol is present in all cell membranes and we would die without it. This study shows that patients, even those with heart failure, need cholesterol for healthy hearts. Nature placed cholesterol in our bodies for a good reason.

Today, it's harder and harder to find patients over 50 years of age who are not taking a cholesterol-lowering drug (CLD). But there's a big unanswered question. Will more of these patients develop heart failure than those who were never prescribed CLDs? There is reason to believe this may be the case because

CLDs decrease the amount of coenzyme Q10 (CoQ10) available for the heart's muscle.

Gas provides the energy that drives our cars. CoQ10 is the energy that keeps the heart's muscle pumping 100,000 times a day. Unfortunately, CLDs can lower the amount of CoQ10 by as much as 40 percent. Good sense dictates that robbing the heart's muscle of its energy is not a wise move unless it's replaced. And most CLD patients that I've seen are rarely advised to take CoQ10.

Fewer cases of heart failure will occur if coronary arteries are kept open by Medi-C Plus™, a powder consisting of high doses of vitamin C and lysine. Studies show this remedy, available at health food stores, reverses hardening of the arteries (atherosclerosis). Healthy and failing hearts last longer if they have a supply of good blood.

Chapter 5 - *Column 1*

Vitamin C and Lysine Powder Help Prevent Heart Attack

Why is heart attack the number one killer in this country? Ninety-nine percent of doctors say it's due to atherosclerosis (hardening of arteries) and that cholesterol-lowering drugs are the primary way to treat it. But I say, it's because cardiologists have closed minds and are ignoring facts that could save thousands of North Americans from coronary attack.

History shows mankind is not kind to new ideas. In 1847, one maternity patient in six who entered the University Hospital in Vienna left in a coffin. Why? Because esteemed professors ridiculed their colleague, Dr. Semmelweiss, for showing them that by simply washing hands after doing an autopsy, deaths were prevented.

Years later, Dr. Linus Pauling, two-time Noble Prize winner, is ignored for reporting that large amounts of vitamin C and lysine are needed to prevent coronary attacks. Twenty-five years ago, Pauling reported that animals make vitamin C while humans do not. That's why sailors died of scurvy during long sea voyages, but the ship's cat survived.

Vitamin C is required to manufacture healthy collagen, the glue that holds coronary cells together, just like mortar is needed for bricks. Lysine, like steel rods in concrete, makes collagen stronger. Pauling claimed it takes a mere 10 milligrams to prevent scurvy, but several thousand to prevent heart attack.

William Stehbens, Professor Pathology at Wellington School of Medicine in New Zealand, proved Pauling was right. Stehbens' research showed that coronary arteries closest to the heart are under the greatest pressure. This causes collagen to fracture resulting in the formation of a blood clot and death.

Dr. Sydney Bush, a British researcher, has now proven that vitamin C can reverse atherosclerosis. Bush took retinal photographs of his patients and then started them on high doses of vitamin C and lysine. One year later, additional pictures showed atherosclerosis had regressed in retinal arteries. This regression also occurs in coronary and other arteries.

So what has happened to these monumental findings? Bush, like Semmelweiss, has been ridiculed by cardiologists. One has to ask whether cardiologists by ignoring his results, are condemning thousands of people to an early needless coronary heart attack.

Fifteen years ago, following my own coronary attack, cardiologists claimed it was sheer madness for me to refuse cholesterol-lowering drugs (CLDs). Instead, I decided to take high doses of vitamin C plus lysine, with breakfast and the evening meal, for several reasons.

I knew that Dr. Graveline, a physician and NASA astronaut, had twice developed transient global amnesia from taking Lipitor®. I was also aware that patients have died from CLDs. Others have developed kidney, liver and muscle complications. I also believed the research of Pauling and Stehbens to be irrefutable. Now, the work of Dr. Bush has convinced me that my decision was prudent.

But to take large doses of vitamin C and lysine requires swallowing many pills daily. It's a tall order for those who dislike swallowing even one pill. So for several years, I've been trying to find a company that would manufacture a combination of vitamin C and lysine powder. Now Medi-C Plus™ is available at health food stores.

The dosage for the Medi-C Plus™ combination is one flat scoop with breakfast and the evening meal, with either water or orange juice. Those at greater risk should take one flat scoop, three times a day. If high doses cause diarrhea, the dose should be decreased.

This column does not recommend that those taking CLDs should stop them. This is a decision that can only be made by patients and doctors.

Most of today's cardiologists are impervious to persuasion. They continue to believe that cholesterol-lowering drugs are the be-all-and-end-all to prevent heart attack. They've been brainwashed by millions of dollars worth of promotion by pharmaceutical companies. It reminds me of the saying that cautions "It's not what you don't know what gets you into trouble, it's the things you know for sure that ain't so!"

It's time for cardiologists to have an open mind and stop ignoring this research. As for me, I bet my life on it.

Chapter 5 - *Column 2*

Common Questions about Medi-C Plus™

The following information is a general guideline. I am not your doctor, always check with your own physician on these matters.

"Why do I have to check with my doctor after taking Medi-C Plus™ for six months?"
This is another bureaucratic government decision that Preferred Nutrition is trying to change. Why? Because to get the benefit of Medi-C Plus™ it must be continued for a lifetime as you cannot produce vitamin C and lysine in your own body. So the regulation makes no sense.

"Can I take Medi-C Plus™ with other liquids?"
Medi-C Plus™ is usually taken with water. You can substitute orange juice, but not grapefruit juice.

"Why hasn't my doctor told me about Medi-C Plus™?"
There are several possible reasons. The main reason is that pharmaceutical companies have spent hundreds of millions of dollars brain-washing doctors that cholesterol-lowering drugs are the be-all-and-end-all to preventing heart attack. So there is little chance your doctor has heard about the research proving that Medi-C Plus™ can prevent and reverse coronary artery disease. History also shows that great medical discoveries are rarely accepted by the medical profession. For instance, Dr. James Lind,

the British naval surgeon, showed that lime juice could prevent scurvy in British sailors. Yet this discovery required another 60 years before the British Admiralty made lime juice available to sailors.

"How will I know Medi-C Plus™ is working?"

You won't know as you cannot see inside your arteries. A highly trained eye doctor, such as Dr. Sydney Bush can see narrowed arteries getting wider after six months of treatment. But you will realize Medi-C Plus™ works when you're 95 years of age and have not suffered from a heart attack or stroke.

"How long must I take Medi-C Plus™?"

You should save your money if you stop Medi-C Plus™ after a few months. Since you will never make your own vitamin C and lysine you must take Medi-C Plus™ for a lifetime to obtain the desired result.

I want to "stop taking cholesterol-lowering drugs, but I'm afraid to do so."

I know of no reason why you cannot take Medi-C Plus™ along with CLDs. After all, you are getting vitamin C and lysine in your food daily without any problems. So adding more vitamin C and lysine should not be a problem. But it is always advisable to discuss this and other medical matters with your own doctor.

"Can I take too much vitamin C and lysine?"

Vitamin C in high doses can cause diarrhea. If this happens, decrease the dose of Medi-C Plus™ to bowel tolerance. But there is no known toxic level to vitamin C or lysine.

"Is there any contraindication to taking Medi-C Plus™?"
Patients who suffer from hemochromotosis, often called iron overload, should not take any type of vitamin C. In these patients, excessive amounts of vitamin C will increase the absorption of iron, which infiltrates many organs of the body and is a serious problem and sometimes fatal. A blood test to determine the level of ferritin can determine if iron overload is present.

"Can I take Medi-C Plus™ with anti-coagulant drugs?"
Large doses of vitamin C can decrease the effect of coumadin and possibly Plavix®. This decision should be made by your own physician.

"I've heard that vitamin C can cause kidney stones."
This is a common misconception. There is no evidence this happens. In fact, some studies show that vitamin C decreases the risk of renal stones.

"Can I take vitamin C if I have a cold or influenza?"
People who have a cold or influenza, or who suffered a trauma, actually have an increased need for higher doses of vitamin C. For instance, animals who develop an infection and normally produce 10,000 milligrams of vitamin C daily will increase the production of vitamin C to 150,000 milligrams.

What is the best age to start Medi-C Plus™?
If I had my life to live over I'd start in my teens. It's logical that the sooner one begins Medi-C Plus™ the less chance of a heart attack, stroke or other cardiovascular complications.

"Medi-C Plus™ does not contain a scoop"
Look harder as it is buried under the powder.

Chapter 5 - *Column 3*

Peewee Amounts of Vitamin C Won't Stop Heart Attacks

How can The Harvard Medical School, my alma mater, be so backward about heart attack? It's apparent its researchers never heard Linus Pauling when he countered critics, with "It's the dosage, stupid". So why is Harvard's study terribly wrong? And how can you benefit from this error?

A Harvard study involved 15,000 healthy male doctors. Half were given a multivitamin pill, the others a placebo. Dr. Howard Sesso of Boston's Brigham and Women's Hospital reported that after 11 years of study, there was no difference between the two groups in rate of heart attacks, strokes, heart failure or chest pain.

What amazes me about the Harvard study is how researchers could waste eleven years studying a project doomed to failure. The multivitamin used contained only 75 milligrams (mg) of vitamin C. This amount is potent enough to prevent scurvy, as only 10 mg is needed to guard against this ancient disease. But prescribing 75 mg of vitamin C to prevent coronary attack is like trying to kill an elephant with a BB gun.

Dr. Linus Pauling reported years ago that it requires several thousand milligrams of vitamin C, along with the amino acid lysine, to prevent coronary attack. Pauling also reminded us that animals produce thousands of mgs of vitamin C daily, but humans lost this ability eons ago. This inability to make vitamin C sets up humans for heart attack and stroke. Increased vitamin C has been proven to prevent this.

Vitamin C makes coronary arteries strong. As mortar binds bricks together, coronary cells are glued together by collagen. But it requires high doses of vitamin C and lysine to produce strong collagen. And just as steel rods provide extra strength to concrete, lysine increases the power of collagen.

Dr. William Stehbens, Professor Pathology at Wellington School of Medicine in New Zealand, reported years ago that Pauling was right. Stehbens emphasized that coronary arteries are under more pressure than any other arteries in the body. After all, they're situated in the heart's muscle, not in the big toe. Moreover, they're under constant pressure while the heart beats 100,000 times every 24 hours, or 37 million times a year, and 2.52 billion times if you live to 70 years of age.

Without sufficient vitamin C and lysine, this constant pounding causes minute cracks in collagen, resulting in blood clots and possible death. Or a weakened artery breaks, causing a stroke.

Dr. Sydney Bush, a British researcher, should be eligible for the Nobel Prize for his finding. Bush took photos of the retina (back part of the eye), then prescribed large doses of vitamin C and lysine. One year later, photos showed that narrowed arteries were gradually restored to normal.

This historic finding is ignored by cardiologists and, sad to say, even by The Harvard Medical School. But medical consumers should benefit from this research when the scientific facts are so valid. I also bet my own life on vitamin C and lysine following a coronary attack 15 years ago. But I hated swallowing so many pills every day.

Fortunately, there's now a combination powder containing high amounts of vitamin C and lysine. Medi-C Plus™ is available at health food stores. A flat scoop of powder contains 2,000 mg of C and 1,300 mg of lysine. It should be taken twice a day with meals, or three times daily if there's a history of heart disease. If diarrhea occurs, the dose should be reduced.

But since I inherited Scottish blood, I hate to see people wasting money. So don't start vitamin C and lysine if it's your intention to do so for only a few months. It won't work. Rather, it's a lifetime habit. Its benefit is being alive at 95 without having suffered a heart attack or stroke. And to my knowledge there is no contraindication to taking vitamin C and lysine along with CLDs.

Chapter 5 - *Column 4*

Eye Examination Can Diagnose Impending Heart Attack

Anne Boleyn, the second wife of Henry VIII, had the misfortune of losing her head. Fortunately, the rest of us still have heads connected to the body, because doctors are increasingly using the eye to diagnose generalized diseases. In fact, detecting early problems through the eye can prevent heart attack, stroke and save legs from amputation.

It's ironic that the human body has 60,000 miles of arteries and veins, the distance of walking two and a half times around the world. But there's only one place where we can see blood vessels, the retina, at the back of the eye, just a square centimeter in size.

Dr. David Ingvoldstad, a U.S. ophthalmologist and authority on retinal disease, says it's not necessary to use invasive procedures to diagnose some generalized chronic problems. The clue is what doctors see when examining the retina.

For instance, a retinal examination may detect small clots in tiny blood vessels. This indicates a stroke may occur if a larger clot blocks blood supply to the brain. Or the detection of inflammation of the optic nerve, along with decreased vision, can point to multiple sclerosis. And, on rare occasions, increased pressure on the optic nerve can diagnose brain cancer.

But the major sign that eye doctors look for is atherosclerosis (hardening and narrowing of arteries) associated with diabetes.

Half of diabetes patients die of heart attack. Others suffer from stroke and kidney failure, or lose legs due to poor circulation from narrowed arteries.

But there is a way to prevent these disastrous complications. However, it is like crying in the wilderness to get the medical profession to accept a vital fact. High doses of vitamin C can both prevent and reverse atherosclerosis.

In writing this column, I feel like the French professor who started a class by saying, "This has all been said before, but must be said again because the last time no one listened." For years, cardiologists have ignored Linus Pauling, Nobel Prize winner, who claimed that humans develop atherosclerosis and heart attack because, unlike animals, they are unable to produce vitamin C or the amino acid lysine.

Cardiologists also refuse to admit that without high doses of vitamin C and lysine, collagen (the glue that holds arteries together) develops cracks where blood clots form, often resulting in coronary death.

It is similarly frustrating that cardiologists have turned a deaf ear to Dr. Sydney Bush, a British researcher. This, in spite of the fact, that he has photos of arteries which show that high doses of vitamin C and lysine can reverse atherosclerosis and save lives.

Fifteen years ago, following a heart attack, cardiologists said I would die when I refused to take cholesterol-lowering drugs (CLDs). Rather, I bet my life on the fact that Pauling was right and opted for high doses of vitamin C and lysine.

This was not a reckless decision. I enjoy being on this planet. And I realize that if I had not become a medical journalist, I would never have met Pauling or had the incentive to study and write about cardiovascular disease. So without this experience, there's little doubt I would have accepted my cardiologists' advice about CLDs. History will prove whether I'm right or wrong.

But I believe that money has driven the sale of CLDs, not good science.

One problem was that I disliked having to swallow so many pills. So I persuaded Preferred Nutrition, to produce Medi-C Plus™, a combination powder containing vitamin C and lysine available in health food stores. The dosage is one flat scoop with breakfast and dinner. Or three scoops daily if there's a history of heart disease. Each flat scoop contains 2,000 milligrams(mg) of vitamin C and 1,300 mg of lysine. If diarrhea occurs, cut back on the dose.

The simple fact is you cannot have good health with arteries clogged by atherosclerosis. Medi-C Plus™ provides the needed Drano. But remember, it's a personal decision of mine to take Medi-C Plus™.

Chapter 5 - *Column 5*

Eight Ways to Decrease the Risk of Heart Attack

Why is it that every 20 seconds in North America someone suffers a coronary attack? It's because the heart is under huge stress, beating every day 100,000 times or 2.52 billion times by age 70. Unfortunately, we can't give our heart two weeks vacation every year. But there are ways to increase the chance your heart will beat longer than 2.52 billion times.

One – Get hooked on fish

Harvard School of Public Health Researchers believes the magic ingredient in fish is omega-3 fatty acids. Fatty acids, like Aspirin®, add oil to the blood making it less likely that blood platelets will stick together forming a fatal clot. They also decrease the chance of ventricular fibrillation (a severe abnormal heart rhythm) causing cardiac arrest.

Two – Then get hooked on an anti-inflammatory diet

We know something is wrong when we develop an inflamed throat. Researchers believe that inflammation also increases the risk of coronary attack and can be predicted by a test called, C-reactive protein (CRP). Dr. Ernst Schaefer, chief of the Lipid Metabolism Laboratory at Tufts University in Boston, says the best way to lower CRP is to lose weight. And to keep away from processed foods, cookies, frozen foods and many dessert items that are high in pro-inflammatory omega-6 fatty acids.

Three – What about cholesterol-lowering drugs?

Readers know I question the role blood cholesterol plays in causing coronary attack and that 99 percent of doctors disagree with me. But if you're attempting to lower blood cholesterol, try natural methods first. Be physically active, have a handful of almonds daily and increase dietary fibre such as oat bran, beans, peas, whole grains, vegetables and fruits.

Before resorting to cholesterol-lowering drugs (CLDs), try natural remedies such as Sytrinol® that consists of citrus and palm fruit extract, known as plant sterols. They help to restore normal levels of blood cholesterol. Sytrinol®, Cholesterol Essentials™ and other brands are available in health food stores and do not share the complicating risk factors of CLDs. Remember, the first rule of medicine is to do no harm.

Four – Coenzyme Q10 to fight congestive heart failure.

It's important to take Coenzyme Q10 if you're taking a cholesterol-lowering drug. CLDs can decrease levels of this enzyme in the heart's muscle by as much as 40 percent. Some authorities worry that this could lead to heart failure later in life, since Coenzyme Q10 is the "gas" that provides energy to the heart.

Five – Aspirin

New evidence shows that taking an enteric-coated Aspirin® is not recommended for those who have never suffered a heart attack. But for those who have had a coronary attack, a daily 81 milligram Aspirin® decreases the risk of another one.

Six – NEO40® fights coronary disease

Nitric oxide (NO) is produced in the endothelium (inner lining) of blood vessels and triggers dilation of arteries. Dr. Nathan Bryan, at the University of Texas, a world authority on NO says that after age 40 the production of NO decreases. This increases the risk of hypertension and the constant pressure causes injury to the inner wall of coronary arteries. The result is an inflammatory reaction that kills one North American every 37 seconds. NEO40® also improves triglyceride levels and is helpful in treating diabetes and asthma. NEO40®, along with an easy saliva test to show your level of NO, is now available in Canadian health food stores.

Seven – Medi-C Plus™ to fight heart attack

Medi-C Plus™ powder contains high doses of vitamin C and lysine. Dr. Linus Pauling reported years ago that large amounts of C could prevent coronary attack. Since then Dr. Sydney Bush, a British researcher, has proved that this combination can prevent atherosclerosis (hardening of arteries) and even reverse the problem. Medi-C Plus™, along with NEO40®, is a potent combination to fight heart attack.

Eight – Alcohol in moderation is one of the best medicines

If you have never abused alcohol, an alcoholic drink before dinner helps to relax coronary arteries. It also increases the "good" cholesterol. As Sir William Osler remarked, "Alcohol is for the elderly what milk is for the young." I'm not going to debate this advice!

Chapter 5 - *Column 6*

How "GAADD" is Slowly Killing North Americans

What happens when you see someone gasp for air and suddenly die from heart attack? It's a scene you never forget. But there's a slow, silent, painless disease called "GAADD" (Generalized Ascorbic Acid Deficiency Disease), a condition that results from a lack of vitamin C. GAADD can lead to blocked arteries, causing not only heart attack, but other serious illnesses. Now, Medi-C Plus™, a high concentration powder of vitamin C and lysine, can prevent this tragedy.

Just as a house needs good plumbing, so does our body require unblocked circulation. There are miles of different arteries to keep clear – a total length of 60,000 miles or 96,500 kilometers.

Dr. Linus Pauling reported years ago that most other animals produce vitamin C, but humans lost this ability eons ago. He believed that fat and cholesterol deposits (atherosclerosis) are caused by low blood levels of vitamin C. This affects our entire arterial system and robs our organs of oxygenated blood.

For instance, the kidneys filter our blood more than 30 times every day. But a steady and growing blockage of renal arteries decreases efficiency, resulting in kidney failure. This means being attached to a kidney dialysis machine several times a week or obtaining a kidney transplant.

Gradual diminution of blood to the eye can also result in disastrous consequences. Tiny arteries carrying blood to nerves of the eye may suddenly shut down causing eye stroke, and loss of vision in the affected eye.

As we age, the possibility of a massive stroke also increases. GAADD may cause blockage of blood to the brain or, because of a lack of vitamin C and lysine, a weakened artery may rupture resulting in paralysis. Lysine, like vitamin C, is not produced in the body. This amino acid provides strength to the wall of arterial vessels, just like steel rods do for concrete.

Today, many males suffer from erectile dysfunction. This condition is due to partial blockage of penile arteries. So no part of the body is immune to GAADD.

It's appalling that in the province of Manitoba, due to inadequate amounts of blood flowing to the legs, 25 percent of all lower limb amputations are done on aboriginal people.

Fifteen years ago, following a heart attack and by-pass surgery, cardiologists said I was mad not to take cholesterol-lowering drugs (CLDs). Instead I decided to take vitamin C and lysine. I believed Pauling more than pharma manufacturers who spend hundreds of millions of dollars to convince doctors and the public of the merits of CLDs.

It was a risky decision because at the time I had never heard of Dr. Sydney Bush, a British researcher. Bush decided to give patients high doses of vitamin C and lysine to see if this combination stopped eye infections in patients using contact lenses. He was shocked to see a year later, that before-and-after photos of the retina (the back part of the eye) revealed that atherosclerosis due to GAADD was gradually fading away.

Since our heads are connected to our bodies, what takes place in the eye's retina also occurs in coronary arteries and all other vessels. Bush should receive the Nobel Prize for this momentous finding.

I visited Dr. Bush in England and saw his amazing photos. I

realized that I had made the right decision to take large amounts of C and lysine. But since I don't like swallowing tons of pills, the supplement company Preferred Nutrition agreed to manufacture Medi-C Plus™, a powdered combination of vitamin C and lysine.

One scoop of Medi-C Plus™ contains 2,000 milligrams (mg) of vitamin C and 1,300 mg of lysine. The recommended dose is one scoop with breakfast and dinner mixed with water or orange juice, but 3 scoops daily for those with a previous heart attack or a family history of heart disease. It's a lifetime treatment.

Some ask, "When will I know if Medi-C Plus™ is working?" Since you cannot see inside your arteries, you won't know. But when you reach 95 years of age and haven't suffered any of the problems I've mentioned, you will know Medi-C Plus™ works.

History shows that new ideas often collect dust. What a shame in this case! Medi-C Plus™ can now prevent needless heart attack and other tragedies caused by blocked arteries. Besides, it's a natural remedy with no known toxicity.

Chapter 5 - *Column 7*

Will President Clinton's Physicians Prescribe Coenzyme Q-10?

I would have given my right arm to be at the press conference following President Clinton's heart surgery. Why? Because I knew that the journalists would ask the same old question. How would the bypass operation affect Clinton's longevity? I also knew his doctors would tell journalists that he would be on cholesterol-lowering drugs for the rest of his life. And I knew that hell would freeze over before anyone asked, "Will the President also be given Coenzyme Q10 (CoQ10) to protect against the adverse effects of cholesterol-lowering drugs (CLDs)?"

Last week in this column, I explained that CLDs have a number of side effects. This column suggests that this country may be facing an epidemic of congestive heart failure (CHF) due to the widespread use of CLDs. Clinton's heart disease presented an excellent opportunity to discuss the merits of CoQ10.

Heart failure is the fastest growing cause of heart disease in North America. Most people relate this to an aging population. Old hearts get tired and become less efficient. But at a meeting in London, England, several researchers suggested a surprising new reason, cholesterol-lowering drugs. It's ironic that the very medication prescribed to prevent heart disease may in fact be causing it!

CLDs such as Lipitor®, Zocor®, Mevacor® and others are effective in decreasing blood cholesterol. But as always, there's a price to pay for drugs.

Cholesterol drugs work by inhibiting an enzyme required for the production of cholesterol. Unfortunately, this enzyme is also needed in the manufacture of CoQ10, an important nutrient for normal cardiac function.

CoQ10 has been called the "sparkplug of our motors". It generates energy for the heart's muscle. And we know what happens when sparkplugs fail to function in automobiles.

Studies show that CLDs, used for one year, can decrease CoQ10 by as much as 40 per cent. This is like draining the gas tank that fuels the car. In this case, it is sapping energy away from the heart and other muscles. Several researchers believe that it is the lack of CoQ10 in the heart's muscle that may be responsible for the increasing rates of CHF.

Currently, 15 published articles show that CLDs lower CoQ10 in humans and how this affects cardiac function. In addition, the higher the dose of CLD, the more CoQ10 is removed from the heart's muscle.

You can bet that President Clinton's doctors will prescribe high doses of a CLD in an attempt to lower his blood cholesterol as much as possible. And my bet is that Clinton, rather than getting an increased amount of CoQ10 to compensate for the adverse effects of the CLD, won't get any at all. There's been no mention of this supplement by his physicians.

Dr. Khursheed Jeejeebhoy, Professor of Nutrition, at the University of Toronto, reports that the heart muscles of patients suffering from heart failure show decreased levels of CoQ10. He also notes that CoQ10 therapy, along with the energy-producing substances Taurine and Carnitine, improves cardiac performance. Several other studies show that patients with heart failure have decreased amounts of CoQ10.

Another report in the American Journal of Cardiology showed

that a daily dose of 150 milligrams of CoQ10 decreases the incidence of angina by 50 per cent. It's believed that CoQ10 allows the heart to work harder before a lack of oxygen causes angina.

Further research shows that as we age, the body's ability to extract CoQ10 from food decreases. Not too surprising, as all our organs work less efficiently with the passage of time.

Printed matter, routinely distributed to patients using CLDs, outlines potential side effects such as muscle weakness and possible liver damage. But no mention is made that CLDs decrease the amount of CoQ10, an action detrimental to the heart.

In 1974, the Japanese government, due to all these findings, approved the use of CoQ10 to prevent and treat heart disease. Today, over 12 million Japanese are taking this supplement.

Several doctors at the meeting in London, England, questioned why pharmaceutical companies have not recommended CoQ10 to counteract the effects of CLDs.

I too wonder why the President's physicians have been so silent about its use. But it would not be the first time a president has received less than the best medical care.

Chapter 5 - Column 8

Vitamin C: What You Don't Know about its Multiple Benefits

I've previously written about how Medi-C Plus™, a powder that contains a high concentration of vitamin C and lysine, can prevent and reverse atherosclerosis in coronary arteries. The combination is a revolutionary discovery. But vitamin C has many other amazing virtues.

Years ago on long sea voyages, up to 90 percent of sailors died from scurvy due to a lack of fruit and its vitamin C content. This vitamin is needed for the production of collagen, the glue that holds cells together. Without C, the body disintegrates as blood vessels rupture causing massive hemorrhage and death.

Just 10 milligrams (mgs) of vitamin C prevents scurvy. But we need several thousand milligrams daily for other medical problems. For instance, millions of North Americans suffer from osteoarthritis. Without sufficient vitamin C to produce collagen, a major component of cartilage, bone eventually grinds on bone. There would be fewer joint replacements if more vitamin C were available to produce healthy collagen.

Rheumatoid arthritis, the inflammatory type, also requires large doses of vitamin C. Every moment of the day, our bodies are using oxygen to keep us alive. But oxidation results in metabolic ash known as "free radicals", which are believed to trigger an inflammatory reaction in joints. Vitamin C is a powerful antioxidant that helps to reduce damaging free-radicals.

Today, billions of dollars are spent annually in North America on cataract surgery. The development of cataracts is a major degenerative disease and an aging population will require more of this surgery. Several studies show vitamin C can slow down the progression of cataracts.

The National Institute of Health reports that macular degeneration, a major cause of blindness, is a nutritional responsive disorder. An NIH study showed that vitamin C taken along with vitamin E, beta-carotene and zinc, could also slow down the progression of macular degeneration.

Vitamin C fights what I've called Generalized Ascorbic Acid Deficiency Disease (GAADD), by decreasing the risk of atherosclerosis, the hardening of arteries.

Every year in this country, leg amputations are performed due to a lack of blood supply causing gangrene of one or both extremities. Others lose eyesight from a blood clot in the ophthalmic artery. It's tragic when a greater awareness of the benefits of vitamin C by doctors could prevent these catastrophes.

The list of health benefits of vitamin C goes on and on. Dr. Robert F. Cathart, an expert on Orthomolecular Medicine says people with asthma have low blood concentrations of vitamin C. He adds that, "A child having regular asthmatic attacks following exercise is usually relieved by high doses of vitamin C."

Corticosteroid drugs are often used to control asthmatic attacks, but long-term use can also cause complications. Studies show that by adding vitamin C to the therapy, the dosage of corticosteroids can often be reduced.

Here is a surprising fact that I wish had known when I developed poliomyelitis during my final year at The Harvard Medical School. Unknown to my eminent professors, a North Carolina physician by the name of Dr. Frederick R. Klenner, treated 60 patients suffering from this disease with massive intravenous doses of vitamin C. None suffered paralysis.

Klenner also discovered that large doses of vitamin C could cure viral pneumonia, hepatitis, chicken pox, measles, mononucleosis, pancreatitis, lockjaw, cystitis and poison ivy.

Vitamin C works by neutralizing viral toxins and stops the formation of new viral units. Or as Dr. Klenner wrote, "Unless our white blood cells are saturated with vitamin C, they are like soldiers without bullets."

I once ended a talk by stressing that C is an amazing vitamin since it cures so many diverse problems. This vitamin has been shown to bolster the immune system, promote healthy gums, guard against mercury and lead toxicity, decrease wrinkles and even neutralize the venom of rattlesnakes.

At the close of the meeting, a friend standing near the exit door could hear the remarks of those leaving. I would have thought that, having discussed how high doses of vitamin C and lysine could protect against life-threatening heart attack and stroke, this would be foremost in the minds of the audience. But I was terribly wrong.

The women were all talking about how vitamin C fights wrinkles!

Chapter 6 - *Column 1*

Sytrinol®: A Natural Way to Decrease Cholesterol

Prescription drugs can kill; natural remedies rarely. It's one of the most important lessons I've learned practicing medicine. So why risk a prescription drug to lower cholesterol when a natural one is available? Sytrinol® can be a safe, effective, less expensive and natural way to lower blood cholesterol and decrease the risk of heart attack.

Cholesterol-lowering drugs (CLDs) do decrease blood cholesterol and the risk of coronary attack. But to question their use is like attacking Motherhood and apple pie, even though there are several short-term and possibly long-term side effects.

For instance, one major study showed that patients taking CLDs may be exchanging one devil for another. Those taking CLDs had 22 fewer deaths from cardiovascular disease, but this was offset by an increase of 24 deaths from cancer. Hardly a good trade!

Researchers at the University of Denmark reported several years ago, that 15 percent of those over age 50 taking CLDs, suffer nerve damage. Dr. Duane Graveline, a superbly conditioned U.S. astronaut, developed transient global amnesia while on Lipitor® and could not recognize his family. He slowly recovered after stopping this medication. Skeptical NASA physicians then prescribed half the dose and his amnesia returned.

Dr Annette Draeger, a researcher at the University of Switzerland, took muscle biopsies from 44 patients on CLDs who were complaining of muscle pain. Her research showed that 57 percent of these biopsies revealed significant muscle damage.

On rare occasions, CLDs can cause rhabdomyolosis, a potentially fatal condition in which large amounts of muscle tissue are destroyed causing kidney failure. For this reason, some CLDs have been removed from the market.

Another, more sinister concern about the long-term use of CLDs, is that they decrease blood cholesterol by inhibiting an enzyme required for the production of cholesterol. Unfortunately, most doctors do not tell patients that this enzyme is also needed for the manufacture of Coenzyme Q10 (CoQ10) – a compound that has been labeled the "spark plug of our motors". It generates energy for the heart's muscle. And we know what happens when spark plugs fail to function in cars.

Studies show that CLDs can decrease CoQ10 by as much as 40 percent. It's like draining the car's gas tank. Moreover, the higher the dose of CLD, the more CoQ10 is removed and therefore, not available for the heart's muscle. A number of authorities believe that by continually robbing the heart of CoQ10, doctors may be setting the stage for a future epidemic of congestive heart failure.

The blunt fact is that consumption of CLDs is not like swallowing candy. They are powerful drugs.

For these reasons, I believe it makes good sense for doctors to at least consider natural remedies to lower blood cholesterol. Sytrinol® consists of citrus and palm fruit extract that contains polymethoxylated flavones (PMFs) and tocotrienols.

Multiple studies show that Sytrinol® decreases total cholesterol by 30 percent, low density lipoprotein (LDL), the "bad" cholesterol by 27 percent, and triglycerides by 34 percent. In addition, high density lipoprotein (HDL), the "good cholesterol" increases 4 percent.

Sytrinol® works by decreasing the oxidation of the bad cholesterol, a factor in plaque formation and narrowing coronary arteries. Sytrinol® also decreases inflammation of arteries which is believed to be associated with increased risk of coronary attack. And by lubricating platelets, the small blood particles responsible for blood clot formation, there's less chance of a clot forming in coronary arteries.

The dose of Sytrinol® is 300 milligrams once a day. It is well tolerated with no reported complications, even when 50 times the regular dose is prescribed. Preferred Nutrition's Sytrinol® is available at most health food stores.

This column does not intend that patients should toss away CLDs. Rather, it's meant to report a natural alternative for lowering blood cholesterol. Patients must not act as their own doctor. But they should be educated about medical matters. So I suggest that readers look at the web site www.sytrinol.net. This makes it easier to make informed decisions about cholesterol along with a doctor.

Chapter 6 - *Column 2*

Non-Toxic Ways to Lower Blood Cholesterol

"Is a natural remedy as effective as cholesterol-lowering drugs (CLDs)?" Or "Is it possible to lower cholesterol by just dietary changes?" These and other questions routinely arrive in my e-mail. What everyone should be asking is, "What is the safest way to lower blood cholesterol?"

Moliere, the French actor and playwright, once remarked that, "Nearly all men die of their medicines, not their diseases." This was a realistic statement nearly four hundred years ago. But, even today in this enlightened age, many people suffer serious and sometimes lethal ends, due to medication. So I always suggest taking drugs the way porcupines make love - very, very carefully. So can you as cautiously lower blood cholesterol?

First, the good news, but only if you're a moderate drinker. An alcoholic pre-dinner drink increases "good" cholesterol. It also lubricates the blood so there's a decreased chance of a blood clot. Moreover, the relaxing effect of a small amount of alcohol does no harm.

There is also good news for the almond industry. Dr. David Jenkins, Director of Clinical Nutrition at St. Michael's Hospital in Toronto, placed 27 men and women with high cholesterol levels on two handfuls of almonds (75 grams every day) for the first month. The next month, they received half the amount.

Jenkins reported that the full dose of almonds reduced "bad" blood cholesterol by 9.4 percent and half the dose by 4.4 percent.

These daily snacks of almonds also resulted in improvements in total blood cholesterol and good cholesterol. Jenkins concluded that two handfuls of almonds could reduce the risk of cardiovascular illness by 20 percent and one handful by 18 percent.

Jenkins also concluded that a change in dietary habits played a role. For instance, the risk of cardiovascular disease was decreased 25 percent when the diet contained cholesterol-lowering foods such as oat bran, barley, psyllium and soy products.

Other studies show that omega-3 fatty acids in fish can help to decrease bad cholesterol and increase good cholesterol.

Few people know that vitamin C decreases blood cholesterol. The best routine is to take up to 5,000 milligrams of ascorbic acid powder (vitamin C) with breakfast and dinner. This converts cholesterol into bile acids that are then excreted in bile to the intestines. Since vitamin C is a natural laxative, it often causes a bowel movement in the morning that removes bile acids before they can be absorbed and converted back to cholesterol. If this high concentration of vitamin C results in diarrhea, the amount should be decreased.

For several years many of my patients have been taking Sytrinol®, a safe, natural, and inexpensive remedy. Sytrinol® consists of citrus and palm fruit extract that contains polymethoxylated flavones (PMFs) and tocotrienols.

Sytrinol® works on cholesterol in a number of different ways. For instance, it blocks enzymes in the liver responsible for the manufacture of cholesterol and triglycerides. It also decreases the absorption of dietary cholesterol.

The polymethoxylated flavones and tocotrienols in Sytrinol® also decrease the oxidation of bad cholesterol. This reduces the risk of plaque formation in arteries and narrowing of coronary arteries. Moreover, by decreasing arterial inflammation and lubricating platelets associated with clotting, there's less chance of heart attack.

Several studies show that Sytrinol® decreases total blood cholesterol by 30 percent, bad cholesterol 27 percent, triglycerides 34 percent, and increases good cholesterol 4 percent.

The usual dose is 300 milligrams (mg) once a day and is well tolerated. Studies show that there are no toxic effects if a 150 pound person consumes 14 grams of Sytrinol® daily. This is 50 times the recommended dose.

The alternative is to take cholesterol-lowering drugs. But I'm sure Moliere would say, "Why chance the risk of muscle degeneration, transient global amnesia, liver and kidney problems, an increased risk of malignancy and possible heart failure if those on CLDs are not taking Coenzyme Q10 as well? It makes more sense to first try this simple, natural remedy.

In my practice, it was rare that Sytrinol® did not work. But I do not suggest that anyone should toss away CLDs. This is a decision that can only be made by your own doctor.

Chapter 7 - *Column 1*

My Personal Vitamin and Mineral Program
IT'S KEPT ME ALIVE!

My Father was a Scot and he taught me to be frugal, but also to buy quality. So since I do not like to spend money foolishly, I've spent many hours thinking about the pros and cons of vitamin therapy as it costs money. I've concluded that for most people, taking vitamins makes sense. The following list comprises the vitamins I take every day and the reason for doing so. There's more than one way to take these vitamins. However, I'm not your doctor and what is good for me may not be beneficial for you. So always check with your own physician before taking any medication or supplement.

Medi-C Plus™ (A Powder of Vitamin C and Lysine)

This is the first vitamin I reach for twice a day. Why? It's because I believe in the work of several outstanding researchers. Dr. Linus Pauling, the winner of two Nobel Prizes, pointed out to me many years ago that although most other animals produce vitamin C, humans do not. This is why sailors used to die of scurvy while the ship's cat survived long sea voyages. Pauling stressed that vitamin C is necessary for the formation of collagen which holds coronary cells together, just as mortar holds bricks together. He believed that, without adequate amounts of C, collagen breaks down and coronary attack results.

Professor William Stehbens, a New Zealand pathologist, later proved Pauling right. He showed that the greatest pressure occurs in coronary arteries when the heart beats. This pressure causes a breakdown of weakened collagen. A blood clot may then form at the site resulting in heart attack. Coronary malfunction also results from narrowed, hardened arteries (atherosclerosis) which cause a decrease in blood supply to the heart. But recent research shows it is possible to improve circulation to the heart's muscle.

Dr. Sydney Bush, a distinguished British optometrist, pre-scribed 6,000 milligrams (mg) of vitamin C to patients who ex-perienced reaction to contact lenses. Luckily, he also took photo-graphs of the retina (the back part of the eye that transmits im-ages to the brain) before the use of vitamin C. He repeated the photographs one year later. To his surprise, the presence of ath-erosclerosis decreased and the retinal arteries were more healthy. Since the head is connected to the body, it's logical to conclude that vitamin C also decreases the amount of atherosclerosis in coronary vessels and supplies more blood to the heart's muscle. Dr. Bush, whose results I have seen firsthand, now has numerous patients proving that atherosclerosis can be reversed. Dr. Bush should get the Nobel Prize for this research. Rather, his out-standing research has been rejected by the cardiology commun-ity and is collecting dust.

It's the old story that new scientific ideas are often rejected and ridiculed by others. Dr. Bush's problem reminds me of what hap-pened to Dr. Semmelweis in Austria 100 years ago. At that time, one in six women in Vienna died in childbirth from infection. Semmelweis showed that when doctors washed their hands after an autopsy, there was a huge decrease in the maternal death rate. But his colleagues ridiculed him to such an extent that his life ended in an institution.

In view of this research by Pauling, Stehbens and Bush, I take Medi-C Plus™, a new combination powder containing vitamin C and lysine with breakfast and the evening meal. One flat scoop contains 2,000 mg of vitamin C and 1,300 mg of lysine. Those who have a family history of coronary heart disease, or who have suffered a heart attack, should take three scoops of Medi-C Plus™ daily. Lysine is an amino acid, which like steel in concrete, provides extra strength to collagen. Since vitamin C is a natural laxative, it can cause diarrhea. It's therefore prudent to start with a lower dose and gradually increase the amount. If diarrhea occurs, decrease the dose to bowel tolerance. Medi-C Plus™ can be taken with water or orange juice. And remember, it's a lifetime regime.

Webber Naturals® Vitamin E

I take 200 mg of natural vitamin E once a day. Vitamin E, like vitamin C, is a major antioxidant that helps rid the body of waste products of metabolism. We all know what happens when oxygen causes an apple to turn brown (oxidation) or steel to rust. Vitamin E helps to mop up the metabolic "ash". It's this leftover ash, known as "free radicals", that is believed to be associated with the aging process, cancer and other diseases.

Recent controversy about this vitamin, namely that it has no effect on preventing cardiovascular problems, may be true but I question this point. Laboratory studies show that vitamin E increases the oxygen-carrying capacity of red blood cells. This means that rats, given vitamin E, can run longer on a treadmill than rats lacking this vitamin. Clinical studies also show that patients who suffer from leg cramps are helped by taking large doses (1,200 IU) of vitamin E. An 80-year-old patient of mine, who had given up tennis due to this condition, took vitamin E and was back on the tennis court two months later. Obviously more oxygenated blood was being delivered to the muscles of his legs.

Vitamin D3

No one knows the ideal dose of vitamin D. Some authorities advise 1,000 International Units (IU) daily while others suggest 5,000 IU. I take 4,000 IU. But one fact is not debatable. People living above the latitude of 35 degrees north which includes Boston, Philadelphia and all of Canada, can stand outside in the noonday sun naked, from October to February, and not manufacture one IU of vitamin D due to the angle of the sun's rays at that time.

Vitamin D has been labelled the "antibiotic vitamin" as studies show it triggers the immune system to fight infections. Dr. John Cannell, a U.S. psychiatrist, published this interesting finding in 2005 when an epidemic of flu struck the hospital for the criminally insane in California. He said those patients taking vitamin D were spared.

Dr. Mitsuyoshi Urashima, a professor of epidemiology in Japan, reported in the *American Journal of Nutrition* that school children given 1,200 IU of D were less likely to develop influenza A than those not receiving this vitamin. He adds that he himself used to suffer several episodes of the flu every year. Now that he takes 3,000 IU daily, he has not had a fever, sore throat or fatigue for two years. The Japanese study also revealed a shocking fact that children not receiving vitamin D, were six times more likely to suffer from asthma.

Dr. JoAnn Manson, Professor of Medicine at The Harvard Medical School, reports that high blood levels of vitamin D help to protect against colon cancer. Other researchers at Creighton University in Omaha, Nebraska, gave 1,200 healthy postmenopausal women 1,500 mg of calcium and 1,000 IU of D to see if this combination decreased the risk of bone fracture. They were surprised to discover that these women were 77 percent less likely to develop cancer, primarily breast malignancy, during the next four years.

Dr. Edward Giovannucci, a researcher at The Harvard Medical School, reports that those with low blood levels of vitamin D were more likely to have a heart attack than those with higher levels of this vitamin. He adds that vitamin D may lower blood pressure, reduce inflammation in arteries and decrease calcification in coronary vessels. Dr Thomas Wang, another Harvard researcher, showed that people with low blood levels of D were more likely to be at risk of not only heart attack but also of heart failure and stroke.

Today, everyone should be aware of the unprecedented epidemic of Type 2 diabetes triggered by obesity. But 10 percent of the population also suffers from Type 1 diabetes due to inheriting bad genes. New evidence shows an increased risk of Type 1 diabetes if there's a deficiency of vitamin D.

Vitamin K2

In 1929, Danish scientist Dr. Henrik Dam discovered vitamin K yet it remains one of the lesser-known vitamins. Today, we know there are two types of vitamin K – K1 and K2. Leafy vegetables are rich in K1 and play a role in blood clotting. But K2 is not easy to obtain in the diet placing many people at risk for this deficiency. Bone, like other tissues, is constantly changing. Cells called osteoblasts build up bone and osteoclasts break it down. During our youth, osteoblasts are dominant, building bone that should last a lifetime. But after age 30, we begin to lose one percent of our bone every year. It's appalling that by age 70, many people have lost 40 percent of their bone mass!

Studies now link Vitamin K2 to the osteoblast which produces a protein called osteocalcin. This protein plays a major role in calcium metabolism. Osteocalcin is like glue. It incorporates calcium into bone, decreasing the risk of osteoporosis and fracture.

Vitamin K2 also plays a major role in the fight against the nation's number one killer, cardiovascular disease. In effect, it places calcium where it belongs, in bones and teeth, and keeps it out of arteries where it causes trouble. Too much calcium in coronary arteries leads to heart attack. Moreover, excessive amounts of calcium make arteries less rubbery and these rigid vessels then set the stage for hypertension, another big killer.

There are some precautions about K2. No one should take K2 if they're using blood-thinning medications such as warfarin or are prone to blood clotting, as this increases the risk of stroke and cardiac arrest.

Vitamin B Complex

B Complex contains a number of the B vitamins. There is evidence that vitamins B6 and B12 help to decrease the risk of heart disease by decreasing the blood level of homocysteine, a by-product of protein metabolism. It's believed that too much homocysteine injures the inside endothelial lining of coronary arteries and sets the stage for heart attack.

Vitamin B12

Are there days when you believe you need a brain transplant because of too many senior moments? It may be because you are not absorbing vitamin B12. This vitamin is firmly attached to a protein and in order to pry it loose so it can be absorbed, there must be sufficient amounts of hydrochloric acid available. Now, we know that one person in five over age 60 and two in five over age 80, can't absorb B12 from food due to a lack of hydrochloric acid.

Studies show that people with high levels of B12 could remember details of short stories better than those with low levels of this vitamin. They were also more adept at listening to a series of numbers and then repeating them backwards. The most effective way to take B12 is by sublingual tablets containing 1,000 micrograms.

Dr. Julian Whitaker's Vision Essentials®

It's been said that, "In the land of the blind, the one-eyed man is king". But wherever you are, good eyes are a priceless possession. Today, tens of thousands of North Americans are unable to read fine print, worry about driving at night or suffer from dry, tired eyes. The best remedy to protect against these troubles is Dr. Julian Whitaker's Vision Essentials®.

Growing older is inevitable, but many of the adverse effects of aging are preventable. Researchers believe that free radicals are a primary cause. To understand their importance, Dr. Whitaker, one of the pioneers of natural remedies, suggests this kitchen experiment. Cut an apple in half, crush a vitamin C tablet, and spread the powder on the cut side of one half. Twenty minutes later, the side protected by vitamin C will remain white and fresh. The unprotected side will turn a dark brown, due to the oxidation process and production of free radicals.

This oxidation process has the same effect on eyes as it has on a sliced apple. To counteract this browning effect on ocular tissues, we need ample amounts of antioxidants such as vitamin C and other nutrients.

"Don't fire until you can see the whites of their eyes" was the famous command given by an American colonel during the Revolutionary War. But if these soldiers had lost their central vision (age-related macular degeneration), they wouldn't have been able to fire a single shot. The macula is a tiny spot in the retina responsible for central vision. Stare someone in the eye at 20 feet and you are looking at the macula. Without a healthy macula, it's impossible to read a book or watch TV. Today, macular degeneration is the leading cause of blindness for those over

50 years of age and affects seven million North Americans.

Vision Essentials® contains 19 of the best antioxidants and minerals known to help aging eyes. They include lutein, zeaxanthin and lycopene to promote the general health of the retina, lens, macula and optic nerve. There's also vitamin C and A, zinc, copper, alpha lipoic acid, taurine, N–Acetyl-L-cysteine, L-glycine and carrot powder. And to sharpen night vision, there's black currant, a natural cousin to blueberries and cranberries.

Just as apples turn brown without antioxidants, so do eyes age without them. Try the kitchen experiment.

Coenzyme Q10

This enzyme provides energy to the heart just as gas supplies energy to cars. We lose the ability to produce CoQ10 as we age. Patients who take cholesterol-lowering drugs, are often unaware that this medication can lower the amount of CoQ10 by as much as 40 percent. Some health authorities believe that if these people do not take CoQ10, they are at risk of developing heart failure later in life.

MINERALS

Magnesium

Studies show that most North Americans are lacking in this important mineral. In fact, magnesium can in some cases, keep the undertaker away. Several years ago, I wrote about an 18-year-old basketball player and health-conscious jogger who suddenly died on the court. The initial diagnosis was thought to be coronary attack. But autopsy eventually proved death to be due to magnesium deficiency. Magnesium has never been a super star mineral like calcium. But magnesium is nature's muscle relaxant. It's amazing that this fact hasn't triggered more attention from the medical community.

In 1979, Dr. J.R. Chipperfield reported in the British journal *The Lancet*, that patients who suffered from angina often had low levels of blood magnesium and that this mineral often eased spasm and pain.

More important, magnesium can prevent sudden death. Regular beating of the heart is controlled by an extremely complex electrical system. Low magnesium levels toss a monkey-wrench into this process causing an abnormal rhythm called ventricular fibrillation. Death may result.

Today, with an aging population, abnormalities in the heart's electrical system often result in auricular fibrillation. This abnormal rhythm increases the risk of a blood clot forming in the heart, travelling to the brain and causing stroke. To prevent this from happening, doctors usually prescribe anti-clotting drugs such as Coumadin® to oil the blood. But this drug has to be finely tuned as too much can cause serious bleeding. I have had several patients who, by taking magnesium, have found their heart beat reverted to a normal rhythm.

Today, few North Americans are getting the required 350 mg of magnesium each day. Tablets are available but MagSense®, a powdered form of magnesium, has several advantages. This product contains not only elemental magnesium, but also calcium, essential amino acids, vitamin E and several B vitamins. The dosage is one tablespoon or scoop daily in five ounces of water.

Calcium

I take 600 mgs of calcium daily to help keep bones strong and decrease the risk of fracture. But as mentioned before, I also take vitamin D (3,000 mg) which helps to absorb calcium. In addition, I take vitamin K2 (100 micrograms) that helps to push calcium into bone where it belongs and keeps calcium out of coronary and other arteries where it does not belong.

Where Do I Buy My Vitamins and Minerals?

I purchase all my vitamins and minerals at health food stores. Medi-C Plus™ is only available in Canada at these stores.

Chapter 7 - Column 2

Vitamin K2 Essential for Good Bones and Hearts

What do the Japanese eat for breakfast that could help North Americans? Every year, 7.5 billion packages of Natto are sold in Japan. The government has made it an integral part of the school breakfast program. Natto contains vitamin K2, a largely unknown vitamin on this continent and it packs a whammy. Studies show that K2 helps to prevent osteoporosis (brittle bones) and cardiovascular disease.

In 1929, Danish scientist Dr. Henrik Dam, discovered vitamin K. Later, Japanese researchers reported that women living in Tokyo, where the centuries-old Japanese food Natto is popular, had increased bone density. But women living in Western Japan, where Natto is not popular, showed a decline in bone density. Further research determined that vitamin K2 in Natto was responsible for this benefit.

Today, we know that there are two types of vitamin K – K1 and K2. Leafy green vegetables are rich in K1 and play a vital role in blood clotting. But K2 isn't so easy to obtain in the diet, placing many people at risk for a deficiency.

Bone, like other tissues, is constantly changing. Cells called osteoblasts build up bone and osteoclasts break it down. During our youth, osteoblasts are dominant, creating strong bone that should last a lifetime. But after age 30, we begin to lose one percent of our bone each year. It's an appalling situation that by age 70 many people have lost 40 percent of their bone mass!

Vitamin K2 has been linked to the osteoblast which produces a protein called osteocalcin. This protein plays a major role in calcium metabolism. Osteocalcin is like glue. It incorporates calcium into bone, decreasing the risk of osteoporosis and fractures.

Japanese studies show that vitamin K2 decreases the risk of vertebral fractures by 60 percent, and hip and non-vertebral fractures by 80 per cent. Other studies show that K2 can increase bone density in postmenopausal women.

But vitamin K2 also fights this nation's number one killer, cardiovascular disease. It places calcium where it belongs, in bones and teeth, and keeps it out of arteries where it causes trouble.

A lack of vitamin K2 triggers a number of cardiovascular complications. For instance, the lack of K2 increases the risk that calcium will be deposited in the aorta. This is the largest artery and carries blood from the heart to the rest of the body. Calcification of the aorta weakens its walls, increasing the risk of rupture and sudden death. A Rotterdam study of 4,600 men aged 55 and older in Holland, showed that a high intake of vitamin K2 decreased the risk of aortic calcification by an amazing 52 percent!

Too much calcium in coronary arteries also leads to heart attack. One study showed that adequate levels of K2 decreased the risk of coronary attack by 41 percent. Moreover, excessive amounts of calcium make arteries less rubbery. The rigid blood vessel then sets the stage for hypertension, another big killer.

Today's headlines rarely mention the increasing number of North Americans who are dying of heart failure. Failure isn't as dramatic as coronary attack, but the end result can be the same. We are all living longer and eventually the heart begins to fail. But it will last longer if calcium is kept in bones and not deposited in heart valves, placing more stress on the heart muscle.

There are some precautions about K2. Don't take K2 if you're using blood-thinning medications such as warfarin, have experienced stroke, cardiac arrest or are prone to blood clotting.

Vitamin K1 is present in leafy vegetables, cheese, olive oil, broccoli, cauliflower green tea and soy beans. Many people are lacking K2 because the major source of K2 comes from steamed and fermented soy beans. No doubt the Japanese like their fermented sticky soy, but it's not what I would enjoy eating every morning.

Preferred Nutrition vitamin K2 contains 100 micrograms of vitamin K2 and is available in most health food stores. The dosage is one capsule daily.

Chapter 7 - *Column 3*

What You Don't Know about Magnesium

"Doctor, am I taking enough or too much calcium?" It's a question I'm often asked by patients. But I can't recall a single instance when a patient has asked the same question about magnesium. It's ironic, as studies show that many North Americans are not obtaining sufficient amounts of this important mineral. In some cases, this can be a fatal error. Now, there's a simple, natural way to prevent this.

Calcium has always enjoyed star status and for good reason. Without sufficient calcium, bones develop osteoporosis in which a minor fall, or a big hug, can snap a bone. But few realize that magnesium is required for more than 300 biochemical reactions in the body.

For instance, a magnesium deficiency can result in hypertension, muscle cramps, restless leg syndrome, diabetes, migraine attacks, emotional trouble, fatigue and an irregular heart rate.

Magnesium is nature's muscle relaxant. But this fact went unnoticed for years. Then in 1979, Dr. J. R. Chipperfield reported in the British medical journal The Lancet, that patients who suffered from angina often had low blood levels of magnesium. He also stated that by prescribing this mineral, the spasm of coronary arteries and pain could be eased.

This important finding prevents heart disease, the nation's number one killer. But, in addition to expanding coronary arteries, magnesium adds oil to the circulation, preventing platelets, the small particles in the blood, from clotting and resulting in sudden death.

Magnesium plays another vital role. Each beat of the heart is controlled by an extremely complex electrical system. Low blood magnesium can toss a monkey wrench into this process, triggering an irregular heart rate called auricular fibrillation. In extreme cases, this can result in ventricular fibrillation and death.

Whether or not you die from a heart attack depends on several factors, such as obesity, hypertension, diabetes and blood cholesterol. But one dilemma, which has been difficult to explain, is why 50 percent of people who die from coronary attack have normal blood cholesterol. Low blood magnesium may be a factor.

The DASH study (Dietary Approaches to Stop Hypertension) showed that this major killer could also be calmed by a diet high in magnesium, potassium and calcium. In another study of 30,000 male health professionals, it was found that the incidence of hypertension was less in those who had a greater intake of magnesium.

A deficiency of magnesium is also fueling the epidemic of diabetes. A report from the University of Virginia showed that a low dietary intake of magnesium is associated with increased insulin resistance. In this study, patients were placed on a diet deficient in magnesium for a mere three weeks. Researchers found that not only did the cells become lacking in magnesium, but also insulin became less efficient in transporting sugar (glucose) from the blood into cells.

Since 1976, Harvard University has carried out a huge study, called the "Nurses Health Study". During this time, researchers followed 85,000 nurses and 43,000 men. They discovered that nurses who consumed 220 milligrams (mg) of magnesium daily were 33 percent more likely to develop diabetes than those consuming 340 mg of magnesium each day.

So how can you get 350 mg of magnesium daily? A good start would be one baked potato with skin 55 mg, one-half ounce of almonds 43 mg, one shredded wheat 40 mg, one cup of plain low fat yogurt 43 mg, one-half cup of brown rice 42 mg, one banana 32 mg, three-ounce grilled salmon 23 mg, one slice of whole wheat bread 24 mg. And don't forget fruits and vegetables.

Since most people don't consume 350 mg of magnesium daily, it's important to use magnesium supplements. Tablets are available from a number of companies. But one company, Preferred Nutrition, has a product called MagSense™, a powdered form of magnesium. It has several advantages as it not only contains elemental magnesium, but also calcium, essential amino acids, vitamin E and several B vitamins.

The dosage is one tablespoon or scoop daily in five ounces of water. This will keep many health problems away and in some cases, even the undertaker. MagSense™ is available in many health food stores.

Chapter 7 - *Column 4*

Vitamin D Therapy: Course 101

A reader remarked, "I remember your column on vitamin D of several years ago. The one that said you could stand out naked all day in winter and never benefit from the sun. What is your current thinking about this vitamin?" Others ask, "How much vitamin D should I take?" Here are the facts you should know about the sunshine vitamin.

One

In the 1900s, researchers discovered that a lack of D caused rickets. The result was bow-legs and knock-knees. Today, this condition is rare due to better nutrition. But reports from Boston show that rickets is on the rise again. For instance, in a study at The Harvard Medical School, 24 percent of teenagers of both sexes aged11 and 18, were deficient in vitamin D. This is a wake-up call. It shows that it's not only the housebound or elderly in nursing homes who are deficient in this vitamin.

Two

Vitamin D's primary function is to maintain normal levels of calcium by helping children and adults absorb calcium from food. This prevents osteoporosis (brittle bones) which is a major cause of fractured bones later in life. Hoarding calcium early in life is like having money in the bank later on.

Three

Dr. Michael Holick, a world authority on vitamin D at Boston University, says vitamin D may play a role in the prevention of breast, colon and prostate cancers. Studies show that cancer rates tend to fall with higher blood levels of vitamin D. Other research even suggests that vitamin D helps to decrease the risk of type I diabetes, multiple sclerosis, Crohn's and Alzheimer's disease.

Four

Dr. Thomas Wang, Assistant Professor, Harvard Medical School, says that heart disease, the number one killer, is linked to vitamin D deficiency. A study shows that Bostonians with low levels of vitamin D were 62 percent more likely to develop heart failure, strokes and other cardiovascular conditions than those with normal levels of D. If patients also suffered from hypertension, they had twice the risk of succumbing to cardiac-related problems.

It should not be surprising that vitamin D decreases the risk of cardiovascular problems. Studies show that this vitamin improves blood lipids and can decrease the risk of blood clots. D also has anti-inflammatory effects and inflammation of arteries is associated with an increased risk of heart attack. A deficiency of D can also trigger the release of extra parathyroid hormone. This, in turn, pulls calcium out of bone and some ends up in coronary arteries, causing blockage and heart attack.

Five

The sunshine vitamin may soon be known as the "Longevity Vitamin". Dr. Harald Dobing at the University of Gratz in Austria reported in *Archives of Internal Medicine* that there is good news for those who yearn to live longer. Patients, who had the lowest blood levels of vitamin D, had twice the risk of dying from all causes, compared to those with the highest levels of D.

Six

But how much vitamin D should you take? The American Academy of Pediatrics recommends that children and teenagers need 400 International Units (IU) daily. For others, most authorities I talked to recommend 1,000 IU of vitamin D every day. But some admitted they were personally taking 2,000 IU daily.

Seven

In addition to the use of vitamin supplements, consider increasing the amount of vitamin D in the diet. Vitamin D is present in salmon, sardines, mackerel and cod liver oil. Today, D is also added to milk and other foods. A cup of milk usually contains 100 IU.

Eight

Coronary heart disease and high blood pressure increase the further you live from the equator. The equator's year-round intense sunlight provides the perfect global condition for the production of vitamin D. But Canadians and those residing in cities such as Boston and Philadelphia live above the latitude of 35 degrees north. From October to February sunlight in these areas hits the earth at an oblique angle. This decreases the ultra-violet radiation that triggers production of vitamin D. This means they receive no vitamin D between October and February. So if anyone feels compelled to stand out naked in the sun, make sure you pick the warmer months and need I add, the right location!

Chapter 7 - *Column 5*

To E or not To E

Should I believe the study that links vitamin E to a possible premature death? I couldn't resolve this question and finally gave up. Possibly I needed a holiday from deadlines as during a cruise along the west coast of Mexico, on Holland America's ship *Ryndam*, the sea air cleared my mind. It occurred to me that researchers had forgotten vital historical facts.

The study causing all the hubbub was a Johns Hopkins report that analyzed 19 clinical trials. It concluded that 400 or more International Units (IU) of vitamin E per day increased the risk of dying from all causes by about four percent. In addition, a Canadian study showed that more people taking vitamin E developed heart failure. So it appeared that taking more of a good thing might not always be prudent.

So vitamin E took a wallop in the press. One newspaper headline was blunt, "High doses of vitamin E can kill you." No wonder that many of my patients stopped taking E. For years, I and other doctors had told them that E had major cardiovascular and additional benefits. Now, I wondered how we could be so wrong.

But cruising in The Sea of Cortez revitalized my brain. The Hopkins study involved many older people with existing chronic disease. How vitamin E affects them may differ from the way it affects healthy persons. But more important, while visiting interesting historical sites in Mexico, I realized that I, along with researchers, had forgotten important historical facts about vitamin E. Ones that cannot be ignored.

Vitamin E was discovered over 80 years ago. Since that time, researchers have conducted many experiments that have collected dust. For instance, when rats were given increased amounts of vitamin E, they could run longer on a treadmill and also survive longer in an oxygen-deficient atmosphere.

Studies show that rats run longer because E increases the oxygen-carrying capacity of the blood, thereby delivering more oxygenated blood to tissues. It's this fact that also helps humans who suffer from intermittent claudication, or pain in the legs.

A 70-year-old patient of mine could only walk a few feet due to leg cramps. He had developed narrowing of the arteries caused by atherosclerosis and his muscles lacked sufficient oxygen. But after a few months of taking vitamin E, he was back playing tennis.

Years ago, it was reported that large doses of vitamin E prevented cataracts in diabetic mice. At a meeting of the New York Academy of Sciences years later, researchers showed that patients who had taken increased amounts of E had similar results. The Harvard Nurses Health Study also showed that 400 IU of vitamin E decreased the risk of cataracts by 56 percent.

In 1994, a Finnish study showed that smokers, who took just 50 IU of vitamin E for five to eight years, had a lower rate of prostate cancer.

Then in 2001, the U.S. National Eye Institute had good news for those suffering from macular degeneration, a major cause of blindness. It reported that vitamin E (400 IU) along with beta carotene (25,000 IU), vitamin C (500 mg), zinc (80 mg) and copper (2 mg) slowed the rate of this debilitating disease.

Vitamin E is also a powerful antioxidant. Every minute of the day, our cells are burning oxygen to provide energy for our body. During this process, free radicals are produced, like the ash that's left over after a fire and E helps to remove this ash. It's believed that free radicals are linked to many aging problems such as cataracts and cancer.

I doubt that researchers could convince my tennis patient to discontinue E. Nor do I intend to stop taking natural E since I believe that history still shows the benefits of this vitamin. Maybe it would help if researchers also took a cruise to Mexico as sea air and historical sites have a way of clearing cobwebs from the mind.

Catchy headlines grab readers. But I deplore sensational ones that portray only one side of the story.

Chapter 7 - *Column 6*

Why the Bear Had the Last Laugh

How much vitamin A are you taking? Not sure? If so, it's prudent to know more about this important vitamin. A report from Tufts University in Boston shows that those who take too much of this vitamin will get more than they bargained for. That's why the bear had the last laugh over Arctic hunters.

Long before researchers discovered vitamins, ancient Egyptians knew that the liver could cure night blindness, the inability to see in low light. Later, Hippocrates prescribed liver soaked in honey for blindness in malnourished children. It's tragic that even today one million children world-wide are blind due to a lack of vitamin A. So adequate amounts of A are needed to prevent this problem, and for reproductive health and immune function.

Today, due to improved diet from eggs, vegetables and the fortification of milk and cereals, there are only isolated cases of vitamin A deficiency in North America. Now, the problem is lack of awareness that it's possible to take too much of a good thing.

Dr. Jeffrey K. Griffiths at Tufts University says, "There is a general belief out there that vitamin A is not only safe in high amounts, but innocuous fundamentally".

But don't try to sell that advice to Arctic hunters. Some unsuspecting hunters tracked down a bear and shot it. Since they all loved liver, they looked forward to a meal of bear's liver and consumed large quantities of it. But, although great hunters, they were "babes in the woods" when it came to knowing about the vitamin A content of bear liver.

Since bears are carnivores, they eat fish-eating carnivores like seals, and consume large amounts of vitamin A. But through evolution, they've developed the capacity to store in their livers 3,000 times the recommended daily amount (RDA) needed by humans. This is why the hunters became violently ill with diarrhea, headache, dizziness and jaundice.

But not only hunters develop vitamin A toxicity. For instance, the RDA for adults is 3,000 International Units ((IU). But for children, the RDA is just 1,000 to 2,000 IU. Several years ago, one company had to recall its energy bars because they contained 32,500 IU of vitamin A!

One young girl developed increasing fatigue, loss of appetite and finally kidney failure. Her grandmother owned a health food store and was gradually killing her with excessive vitamin A. Another child developed agitation, fever and pains in her bones due to vitamin A poisoning.

Adults who receive too much vitamin A complain of hair loss, nausea, dry, scaly skin, fatigue, headaches and blurred vision.

So how much is too much? Authorities say that chronic toxicity can occur by taking 25,000 IU. But in the 1990s, it was discovered that even low levels could put people at risk. Women taking the drug Accutane®, a derivative of vitamin A used to treat acne, were more prone to having children with birth defects such as heart problems or cleft palate.

Excessive amounts of vitamin A have also been linked to hip fractures. The Harvard Health Study has followed 120,000 nurses for the last 26 years. Researchers reported that postmenopausal nurses who consumed 10,000 IU of vitamin A had a 48 percent greater risk of hip fracture than women who consumed 1,250 IU vitamin A.

This association has been confirmed by another study in Sweden where cod liver oil is traditionally used as a natural remedy to prevent disease. In this study, women who consumed 5,000 IU of vitamin A daily had double the number of hip fractures compared to those with intakes of about 1,650 IU.

The Harvard study also revealed that some nurses obtained 40 percent of their vitamin A from multivitamin tablets. So if you're getting vitamin A this way, be sure to read how many IU's are in the tablet.

The message is that not all vitamins play by the same rules. For instance, vitamin C is water soluble, easily used up, excreted from the body and has no toxic level. But A is fat soluble, stored in the body and potentially dangerous for hunters and the rest of us.

Chapter 8 - *Column 1*

Fighter Pilots: Can You Pass Their Test?

I've often wondered who the most interesting person was of all those I've interviewed over the last 37 years? It's a tough decision. After all, how do you eliminate a two-time Nobel Prize winner like Linus Pauling? Or the discoverer of the Aids virus? Or The Queen of England's personal physician. But in these recent black days my mind has returned repeatedly to Dr. Thomas Hackett, a professor of psychiatry at The Harvard Medical School. In these post-Bin Laden times, see if you flunk or pass this quiz.

We all have various hobbies. But I would have liked to have accompanied Dr. Hackett as he relentlessly pursued his interest year after year. His passion? Tracking down World War I fighter pilots.

Why fighter pilots? As a psychiatrist he wanted to see if they possessed a certain mental and emotional quality that helped them survive the stress of battle one-on-one. And whether this attitude also aided them later on in life.

It was not an easy nor inexpensive task finding these pilots. He did it by travelling thousands of miles during vacations and finally interviewed 40 of them.

Fighter pilots in World War I faced horrendous odds. One in four were killed in training when unreliable planes crashed during take-off. Once in combat their average life span was a mere three to six weeks. Only one in 20 survived the war.

So why did pilots accept this risk? They told Hackett they were either bored, convinced the Germans must be stopped or had heard French women were beautiful!

But Hackett discovered it was more than their love for glamorous French women that set these pilots apart from others. He explained that the great quality they possessed was a "wealth of optimism and a want of fear".

These were traits he observed over and over as he talked to the men. They also shared a sense of humour and an ability to reduce or abolish fear and worry even in times of great stress. As Hackett remarked, "they could turn off the juice".

Denial, either conscious or unconscious, was fundamental to their defense mechanism. In effect, the pilots saw themselves as indestructible. Equally important, this attitude of being invulnerable continued long after they left the air force.

Hackett's study of fighter pilots revealed other traits. They were all obsessed with fitness. As young adults they had all been athletic and had continued to stay in good physical shape throughout their lives.

They told Hackett that their mothers were not their motivating factor. The majority wanted to emulate their fathers. And it was amazing that none of the 40 families had been split by divorce.

They had all married, one at 76 years of age. 75 percent had been married twice, most often within a year of the death of a spouse. And they all took vacations to exciting and unusual places.

Alcohol had been a problem for only three of the pilots. But each had been able to stop drinking. They had all smoked at one time, but everyone had either quit or greatly reduced this habit.

One would have thought that surviving one-in-twenty odds of death by aerial combat would have made them very religious.

But only six of forty went to church.

Having survived the war they refused to take foolish risks. They developed this trait during the war spending hours oiling their guns. They knew a jammed gun meant death. This had also made them cautious in business, only investing when risk could be minimized.

None of the pilots ever suffered from psychiatric illness. Four admitted to depression on the death of a spouse. But they all refused to seek help and recovered in time.

What happened when they became ill? They denied being frightened, displayed a fatalistic attitude and minimized the seriousness of the disease. And they overcame adversities such as the stock market crash of 1929.

Today in these terrorist times we should strive to develop the fighter pilot's philosophy of "a wealth of optimism and a want of fear". And I'm sure they would all pass a test used by Dr David Rosen who specializes in stress management.

So here goes; Take a look at these letters, "opportunityisnowhere". If you decipher the letters to read "opportunity is now here" you will survive disastrous times. But you flunk the test if you read, "opportunity is no where".

Chapter 8 - *Column 2*

I'll Loan You My Daughter if This Doesn't Worry You!

What can we learn from history as we start 2005? Thirty years ago I filed away an article and forgot about it. An editorial in The Ontario Medical Review claimed that people were becoming obsessed with health. It suggested that if the U.S Declaration of Independence were written today it would declare that it was the pursuit of health, rather than the pursuit of happiness, that would be the third inalienable right of Americans. Another old clipping reminded me of Kissick, his law and his daughter.

The OMR article written by Dr. Samuel Vaisrub claims that years ago people tended to disregard symptoms, fight off problems themselves, were lackadaisical about disease prevention, and doctors had to prod people to look after their health. Now, Dr. Vaisrub claimed, people were obsessed with their health. And this was 30 years ago. Now this obsession has reached epidemic proportions.

It's obvious what has triggered this paranoia. We are bombarded daily with health data by the media. There's a staggering list of over-the-counter pills, health food, vitamins and the ever-expanding list of prescription drugs. And we are warned to ignore them at our peril.

Nothing seems to be normal these days. For instance, a recent report from Tufts University warns that even "normal" blood pressure may be too high. And physicians are constantly being told to reduce their patient's blood cholesterol levels lower and lower.

All this is having profound effects on our psyches and also on health care in North America, which brings us to Kissick's Law. Thirty years ago Kissick, a professor at the distinguished U.S. Wharton School of Business, stunned Canadians with a show-stopping speech about the economic laws of health-care economics. Obviously, considering the huge health-care mess today, Kissick's message was soon forgotten.

Kissick warned that no society in the world has sufficient money to provide all the health services its population is capable of using. And if the current trend of spending more and more of the nation's finances on health care continues it would soon consume the nation's entire budget.

He added that even if 100 percent of the nation's gross national product was spent on health care it would still be unable to meet the population's voracious appetite for medical treatment. He said the problem was similar to giving his American Express Card to his daughter and saying "darling go out and buy anything you want and I will pay all your bills". And if this did not alarm anyone in the audience he would loan them his daughter!

As I looked at these two old, dusty articles, I concluded that we are indeed approaching the time when we will be forced to accept a basic fact. That man cannot live for health care alone. If our collective psyche refuses to accept that conclusion then blunt economics will finally decide it for us. After all, we'd have to leave some money for roads, sewers, education and numerous other necessities of modern living. We also have to leave enough money to keep our economic system competitive in an increasingly competitive world.

I often ask patients if they know the definition of a "well patient". I get a variety of answers. The definition I give them is

"It's a patient who has not seen enough doctors or had enough tests done." They know I'm being facetious but I want to drive home a point. Today, so many tests are available that if enough are done they'll be sure to find something amiss.

So as we enter 2005 let's try to be less obsessive about health. The human body is an amazing organism and superbly designed to last for many years. But only if it's not abused with cigarettes, alcohol and drugs both legal and illegal that many patients don't need, lack of exercise and excessive pounds.

If we remain obsessive what will happen? Another imaginative doctor writing 30 years ago also made a prediction. He concluded that "In the end we will all become doctors spending our time screening each other for disease!"

My best wishes for a happy and healthy, and not too obsessive, 2005

Chapter 8 - *Column 3*

Heroin for Terminal Cancer Patients

Never had I encountered such lies, half-truths, scheming and hypocrisy as happened to me in 1979. I knew that heroin had been available in England for 80 years to ease the suffering of terminal cancer patients. So I wrote a column pleading for its legalization in Canada. I thought it would be looked on as a humanitarian endeavor. But I forgot one vital point. The Canadian Cancer Society (CCS), doctors and other therapists don't like to be told they have been wrong for 80 years! Or as Voltaire wrote, "It is dangerous to be right when the government is wrong".

This column opened a "Pandora's box" and the establishment fired their big guns at me. The CCS labeled me a "headline-seeking journalist" and argued that "morphine was as good as heroin most of the time". But what if you were not one of those "most of the time patients"? Heroin has been proven to be the most potent painkiller. But time and again the CCS shot themselves in the foot with such idiotic remarks. Pharmacists and the RCMP also worried about security of the drug and I received no support from the Canadian Medical Association.

This criticism was unadulterated nonsense. Ask addicts about the potency of morphine vs. heroin and they look at you as if you are crazy. Heroin is much stronger than morphine, penetrates the blood brain barrier quicker and provides a euphoric feeling, easing anxiety.

During my research I visited The Great Ormond Street Hospital for Children in London, England where nurses told me "heroin gives dying children a fuzzy feeling". Besides, dying cancer patients are often emaciated with few areas left to inject painkillers. Since heroin is stronger, a smaller amount can be injected causing less pain.

Although critics wanted to burn me at the stake, readers supported me. At one point I delivered 40,000 letters in several large green garbage bags from readers whose loved ones had died of cancer to the Minister of Health in Ottawa. I said to the Minister, "Never before in history have garbage bags delivered to Parliament such a consistent reaction to a single issue, a stinging indictment of political bureaucracy and such a heart-rending story of human suffering".

Finally politicians were forced by public opinion to establish an Expert Advisory Committee to study the effectiveness of heroin, a total waste of time. Several committee members were opponents of heroin and it was like putting the fox in charge of the henhouse. Their decision was immediate that this demon drug should not be legalized for the dying.

While this was going on I also presented a brief to the Committee on Health. At that time I explained that the witnesses that I wanted to present were not able to attend. They were all dead.

To see first-hand the situation in England and Scotland I visited these countries and talked to a variety of health and law enforcement agencies such as Scotland Yard. All authorities stated that security was not a problem. No masked criminal had invaded a pharmacy with a machine gun.

British health experts stressed another point, that North Americans should stop worrying about patient addiction. For instance, patients could be prescribed several hundred milligrams of heroin, but if they experienced a remission of the cancer, they could be weaned off heroin in two to three weeks. When taken for pain the addictive qualities of heroin are consumed.

In April 1983 I established the W. Gifford-Jones Foundation and asked readers to donate money to continue this campaign. I received several thousand dollars which was used to mount a concentrated and unrelenting attack on those opposed to this legislation. Eventually full page ads and letters from angry readers to members of Parliament won the day.

I later discovered, to my shock, during a visit to the World Health Organization (WHO) in Geneva, Switzerland, that a senior medical officer at WHO said Canada could have obtained a permit to use heroin for medical reasons simply by asking for one! If *the* government was aware of this they were perpetuating a cruel, senseless and unconscionable position against the dying for years.

On December 20, 1984 heroin was legalized for the treatment of terminal cancer patients. I had given doctors heroin on a silver platter. But it was a battle won and a war lost. Many hospitals required doctors to obtain a committee's approval before using it so few bothered to prescribe. Finally the pharmaceutical company discontinued the importation of heroin.

Today cancer specialists continue to betray their patients who experience agonizing death, a tragedy that need not happen.

In 1998, I terminated the W. Gifford-Jones Foundation and gave the remaining $500,000 to the University of Toronto Medical School to establish the Gifford-Jones Professorship in Pain Control and Palliative Care.

Chapter 8 - *Column 4*

Rx for the Heart: Marry a Smart Woman

Thank God, I married a smart woman. And one who majored in English. Commas, colons and semicolons are a puzzle to me. I'd still be puzzled, were it not for her, wondering whether to use "a" or "an", "affect" or "effect", "escapee" or "escaper". I'll die before I know the meaning of a compound noun. This column wouldn't have lasted one year if I'd married a not-so-literate wife. But, just as important, I might have died long ago from heart disease. A new study shows that marrying smart is good for the heart.

Investigators from the Institute of Nutrition Research at the University of Oslo, Norway, analyzed 20,000 married men over a 14-year period. The men, ages 35 to 56 years, were part of a study looking at a number of risk factors for cardiovascular disease.

Researchers obtained information about their cholesterol levels, blood pressure, smoking habits, weight and exercise routine. They were asked if they had a history of heart disease or angina and if they were taking medication to decrease blood pressure.

But these researchers prodded further. They wanted to know which men had married bright women and which ones had walked down the aisle with a not-so-well-educated bride.

Out of the 20,000 men, the wives of 6,000 were less educated than their husbands, while 5,000 wives were better educated and the rest had similar education levels.

The results showed that the men with intelligent wives had the jump on cardiovascular disease. They had lower blood cholesterol, smoked less, exercised regularly and were less likely to be overweight.

But how does all this brilliance in women affect (or is it effect) us men? Dr. Haakon Meyer, the main investigator, provides the answer in the *International Journal of Epidemiology*. He says that our wives make all the decisions about food and family lifestyle.

In the majority of households, women decide what goes into the supermarket cart. Will it be homogenized or skim milk? Will it be loaded with cookies and soda drinks containing sugar? Will they choose any vegetables? Will there be more fish or more meat in the basket? And which cooking oil will they choose? In the end, Dr. Meyer reasons that better educated women make healthier decisions.

Now in the clear light of dawn, I wonder why Dr. Meyer had to study 20,000 married men to know what every man already knows – that wives have always made such decisions for us. But how many of us knew it would save us from coronary attack?

Some readers who know I had a heart attack four years ago might be saying, "Why didn't your wife's intelligence help you? Or maybe she's not that bright." But it's wiser to conclude that without her, I might have had a coronary 20 years earlier.

If you've been lucky to marry a smart woman, there's an additional benefit. She's not only going to live longer but also stay smarter longer.

Researchers at the University of Leiden in the Netherlands, studied 599 men and women, a combination of married couples, unmarried, widows and widowers, all aged 85. They discovered that the women were mentally quicker and sharper than the men. In word and number recognition tests, the women gave speedier responses. They also beat the men in memory tests.

But another and more disturbing finding for men surfaced. Researchers found that 70 percent of the women tested had had little education while more than half the men were well-edu-cated. Yet the men still lost out to the women!

Investigators concluded that social factors did not account for this difference in intelligence. Rather, that men lost out biologic-ally. It was a polite way of saying (in these proper times when we cannot profile anyone) that women were born smarter than men.

Do I feel depressed with this finding? Not at all. I can live with the fact that my wife knows what a compound noun is and I never will. Or hearing her say, "You can't say that in your column!" After all, if she had allowed me to say everything I wanted to say, I'd probably be standing in the dock. So I say, "Amen, and thank heaven for smart wives."

Chapter 8 - *Column 5*

We Need a Boar's Head Pub in Every Hospital

How about opening an English-style pub in your local hospital? Just mention this idea to a hospital board and it will question your sanity. Readers may also conclude that I've gotten into the sauce while writing this column. But 25 years ago, I visited the Boar's Head Pub in Toronto's Sunnybrook Veterans' Hospital and left convinced that it helped patients cope with medical problems better than most medications.

Today, hardly a week goes by without hearing that a common drug is causing heart attack, stroke or some other serious complication. Look at any medication and its literature lists potential complications as long as your arm. Alcohol, on the other hand, is one of the oldest drugs known to man and a more useful one, if used with moderation.

I've never forgotten the Boar's Head or Sheila, the personable barmaid. The pub was licensed by the Liquor Control Board of Ontario and the Royal Canadian Legion provided the funds for the project.

Sheila didn't have a degree in psychology, but was loaded with practical savvy and communicated with patients better than most physicians.

One patient became extremely depressed upon hearing his leg required amputation. He was finally persuaded that a glass of beer at the pub might help to relieve his anxiety. That's when Sheila started her therapy, just by listening to his fears. She convinced him to return the next day, introduced him to other patients and eventually to one who had lost both legs. Seeing how he had coped, along with the camaraderie of the pub, helped to restore his confidence.

I watched how Sheila charmed those suffering from a variety of illnesses that had disrupted their lives. She welcomed them with, "Hi, George, your usual?" Or "What's the matter, Charlie? Did the nurses turn you out of your room?" It always brought a smile. So did the little kiss on the cheek when she delivered the drink to those who had lost limbs. Sheila said it was not part of her job description, but it showed someone cared. Today, she would be fired, accused of sexual harassment.

The pub's drawing force was not just beer. Some patients dropped by for a soft drink or merely to talk to other patients. It was a chance to escape the boredom of hospital routine.

A look at Sheila's scrapbook revealed how she had affected many lives. Grateful letters arrived after some had left the hospital. One 82-year-old man presented her with a daring black negligee. Today, he'd be in trouble.

The pub did not encourage alcoholism. Patients whose medical condition permitted an alcoholic beverage were issued pub cards. This entitled them to two drinks a day and visitors the same number.

I recall shocking nurses when I ordered an alcoholic drink for a patient a couple of days after surgery, if the patient previously enjoyed a pre-dinner drink. Why not? A single drink before eating never killed anyone. Besides, alcohol oils the blood, making it less likely to form a clot, relaxes blood vessels, increases the good cholesterol and improves appetite. This order also helped to convince patients that I didn't think they were going to die.

Critics argue that a hospital pub will increase alcoholism, counteracting any medical benefit. There will always be those who abuse such privilege. But people who drive cars at 140 miles an hour kill others and we don't ban the sale of cars.

Regrettably, the Boar's Head has closed. Hospital patients can no longer look forward to a Happy Hour at the end of the day. And I'm sure hell will freeze over before a hospital board in this country has the imagination to start another one.

The alternative is that patients are confined to looking at four walls, day after day. Rather than providing those who desire it with a relaxing alcoholic drink to brighten their day, doctors now knock them out with tranquilizers and questionable sedatives. Visit a chronic care facility and see it firsthand. Then decide which medication you would prefer.

Remember that God turned water into wine. I'll bet he had a good reason. What do you think about a pub in every hospital?

Chapter 8 - *Column 6*

New Treatment for the Fractured Male Organ

"So you're the doctor who wrote that column!" I'm still greeted by that remark even though it's 11 years since I first wrote about "The Fractured Male Organ". I know doctors shouldn't make light of a patient's medical problems. But I couldn't stop chuckling when I first researched this malady. Now there's a new treatment for this embarrassing problem.

A man was admitted to the emergency department at 1:00 A.M. in obvious distress. He was agitated, his skin cold and clammy, all signs suggestive of blood loss. Doctors were shocked to find a markedly swollen penis as the cause which required immediate surgery to remove a large blood clot.

The $64.00 question – how did it happen? He was reluctant to explain, but finally admitted he had been masturbating vigorously when he heard a sudden snap followed by intense pain and swelling. The diagnosis? A fractured penis, the 67th case to be reported in world literature. But it was how other cases occurred that amused me.

One Romeo was making love to his partner standing up. He must have been one hell of a lover because she suddenly fainted. This sudden, precipitous fall fractured his organ.

A 26-year-old man's honeymoon came to an abrupt halt. He became so overwhelmed with passion during sex that his penis struck his bride's hard pubic bone. Both parties heard a sudden clicking sound and then stared in utter amazement at the bent penis. Another newlywed fractured his organ while rolling over in bed during an erection. What a horrendous way to start a honeymoon!

Dr. Ashraf, an English urologist, reported on several other cases in the *Journal of Urology*. One of his patients was an 18-year-old shepherd who was in a tree watching his sheep. But alas, he fell asleep and his mind must have wandered to pretty girls. He developed an erection, fell out of the tree onto a wooden bar, and another snap occurred.

One Casanova was romancing his partner in a moving car. But during intercourse, the car suddenly stopped. He was tossed against the dashboard with the same result. Another man slammed his penis in a car's door. This sure takes considerable skill and planning! Still others bumped into chairs or beds during the night.

The majority of cases require pressure dressings, anti-inflammatory drugs, sometimes surgery. Tranquilizers are usually needed to calm these terrified males and, needless to say, they're cautioned not to have an erection for several days! Ninety percent of men are left with an upward angle to the penis which causes pain and makes sex difficult. That's no laughing matter.

The first case of penile fracture was described by the physician to King Louis XIV. And some doctors believe this condition is more common than previously suspected.

Dr. Olisa Awogu, a urologist at Southend Hospital in Essex, England, recently spoke to the American Urological Association. He presented 31 cases of men suffering from this condition and how the bent penis can be helped by shock wave therapy.

Shock wave therapy (lithotripsy) has been used for several years to break up kidney stones, to treat tennis elbow and plantar fasciitis, a painful heel condition. Now, Dr. Awogu reports that lower doses are helping many patients with a scarred bent penis.

Several of his patients now have a straight organ. Others have less of an angle.

Dr. Robert Gordon, a Toronto surgeon, and shock wave specialist, says the success rate for decreasing the angle is about 28 percent. But it's of great help in easing pain during an erection.

Since preventive medicine is always better than cure, there are some lessons to be learned from this misfortune. It's invariably safer to lie down while making love. But if great lovers think otherwise, they must be prepared to catch the fair damsel if she suddenly faints. You must never, never make love in a moving car. Keep a flashlight at the bedside to avoid obstacles. And I'm sure the shepherd now keeps one eye open while watching his sheep.

This column resulted in me being quickly fired by 7 newspapers in the U.S. bible belt! Unfortunately some people have no sense of humour. In Canada one editor, who normally looked at my column prior to publication, and failed to do so, nearly got fired by the publisher. But his job was saved when a flood of readers called the newspaper saying it was the best column they had ever published.

One angry farmer contacted me saying, "Gifford-Jones you may think this problem is humourous, but you wouldn't be laughing so much if this had happened to your prize bull".

Chapter 8 - *Column 7*

Rx Ha Ha

A Russian youth, a member of the Siberian Ski patrol, arrived home after guarding the frontier for several months. He was asked by a TV interviewer, "What do you do first on arriving home after being away for so long?" He replied, "I make love to my wife". The interviewer replied, "I understand that, as you've been away a long time. But what do you do next?" The young man replied, "I make love to my wife again." "Yes", the frustrated interviewer continued, "but then what do you do?" The young Russian replied, "Oh, I take off my skis."

Some readers may be thinking, "Don't sell the farm if you plan to be a comedian." But I do hope that at least this joke made some of you laugh because studies show a good "Ha Ha" is one of the best medical treatments.

Dr. Robin Dunbar, an evolutionary psychologist at the University of Oxford in England, says that animals groom, pat and delouse one another to develop bonding. Humans fortunately don't have to delouse one another, but Dunbar claims our social chuckles are "grooming from a distance".

Dunbar says that a hearty Ha Ha also increases endorphins, morphine-like substances that help to decrease pain.

To prove his point, he showed participants a number of different videos, some of which were comical. First, he slipped a frozen wine sleeve over their forearms or tightened a blood pressure cuff to test their pain threshold. This showed that laughing at funny scenes did decrease the amount of pain.

Many years ago, Norman Cousins, a former editor of the *Saturday Review* magazine, developed a crippling joint disease following a stressful trip to Europe. His doctors told him he faced a grim future.

Cousins decided to see if laughing could affect the course of his illness. Day after day, he watched old movies of comics Laurel and Hardy. He discovered that after 10 minutes of laughter, he could sleep without pain for two hours.

Cousins' doctors at the University of California were so impressed with his recovery that for many years he lectured to medical students on what he called, "The muscular benefits of internal jogging without having to go outdoors."

A good belly-laugh also provides such a good workout for abdominal and chest muscles that when laughter and muscles relax, the heart rate and blood pressure drops. This calming effect lasts for 45 minutes.

A hearty chuckle also produces nitric oxide which relaxes arteries and helps to decrease blood pressure. In a recent column, I mentioned how a new product NEO40® also produces nitric oxide and by dilating blood vessels, helps to fight fatigue, cardiovascular disease, diabetes, arthritis and other conditions. See the web site www.neogenis.com

Laughter can't cure everything. As one man remarked, "Those who say that laughter is the best medicine never had gonorrhea." And if you have diabetes, you need insulin to live.

But down through the ages, laughter has helped to ease much emotional pain. Abraham Lincoln once remarked during the U.S. civil war, "With the fearful strain that is on me night and day, if I did not laugh I would die."

Today, more than ever, we need more Ha Ha in this troubled world. As Alan Alda remarked, "When people are laughing, they're generally not killing one another." They are also not getting as ill as unhappy people. And as Sir Max Beerbohm, the British actor remarked, "Nobody ever died of laughter."

So let's have one last attempt this week to increase your health by having a good Ha, Ha.

Doctor to his patient, "You're in good health and you'll live to 80". Patient, "But doctor, I'm already 80 years old." Doctor, "See what did I tell you?"

Then there's the story of the man who was walking past a wooden fence at the insane asylum and heard all the residents chanting "13, 13, 13". The man, curious to know what was happening, looked for a small hole in the fence and peeked in. Immediately, he was poked in the eye and everyone in the asylum started chanting "14, 14, 14".

Enjoy the week. Have a good laugh.

Sign up for my FREE health tips at www.docgiff.com